ADAPTIVE WEB DESIGN

Crafting Rich Experiences
with Progressive Enhancement

by Aaron Gustafson
Foreword by Jeremy Keith

SECOND EDITION

Adaptive Web Design, Second Edition
Crafting Rich Experiences with Progressive Enhancement
Aaron Gustafson

New Riders
Find us on the Web at www.newriders.com
New Riders is an imprint of Peachpit, a division of Pearson Education.
To report errors, please send a note to errata@peachpit.com

Copyright © 2016 by Aaron Gustafson

Acquisitions Editor: Nikki Echler McDonald
Production Editor: Tracey Croom
Development Editor: Stephanie Troeth
Copy Editor: Kim Wimpsett
Proofer: Patricia Pane
Compositor: Danielle Foster
Indexer: James Minkin
Cover Design: Veerle Pieters
Interior Design: Ben Dicks
Technical Editors: Chris Casciano, Craig Cook, and Steve Faulkner

ISBN 13: 9780134216140
ISBN 10: 0134216148

9 8 7 6 5 4 3 2 1

Printed and bound in the United States of America

For Kelly

ACKNOWLEDGMENTS

Without the mentorship and assistance of so many of my friends and colleagues in this industry, not only would this book have never been written, but I would not have been in a position to write it. I'd like to take a moment to extend them my sincerest gratitude.

To Molly Holzschlag and Jeffrey Zeldman for taking me under their wings and helping me hone my skills as both a speaker and writer. And to the numerous conference organizers and publishers who've given me the opportunity to apply those skills.

To Steph Troeth for helping me organize my thoughts and the flow of this book. Her support, encouragement, and mangement of this project made the whole experience incredibly fulfilling and—dare I say—enjoyable!

To Chris Casciano, Craig Cook, and Steve Faulkner for keeping my code on the straight and narrow, highlighting my oversights, and ensuring I explained complex topics both simply and clearly. Their contributions were incredibly thoguhtful and appreciated.

To Tim Kadlec, Jeremy Keith, and Ethan Marcotte for reading my early drafts and saying such nice things about them.

To Veerle Pieters for making time in her busy schedule to update the look and feel of this book and design me an even more beautiful cover than she did for the first edition.

To Ben Dicks for his fantastic work on the interior layout and all the custom illustration work.

To Jeff, Matt, Adam, and the rest of the Perma team for creating a system to maintain web citations in perpetuity and for allowing me to add the links I referenced to their permenant collection.

To the fine folks at Pearson/New Riders: Nikki McDonald for championing this book's move to Pearson and Tracey Croom and Mimi Heft for their invaluable help with the production of the book.

And, of course, to Kelly, for granting me the time to write this book, keeping me focused, and pushing me to get it done.

ABOUT THE AUTHOR

As would be expected from a former manager of the Web Standards Project, Aaron Gustafson is passionate about web standards and accessibility.

In his nearly two decades working on the Web, Aaron has worked with a number of companies you've probably heard of, including Box, Happy Cog, Major League Baseball, McAfee, *The New York Times*, SAS, StubHub, the U.S. Environmental Protection Agency, Vanguard, Walgreens, and Yahoo. He joined Microsoft as a web standards advocate to work closely with their browser team.

Aaron loves to share his knowledge and insights in written form. His three-part series on progressive enhancement for *A List Apart* is a perennial favorite and his seminal book on the subject, *Adaptive Web Design*, has earned him numerous accolades and honors. When he's not writing, Aaron is frequently on the road presenting at conferences and running workshops across the globe.

Back home in Chattanooga, Tenn., Aaron is the proprietor of the Chattanooga Open Device Lab and helps organize the Code & Creativity talk series with his partner Kelly McCarthy. He is a longtime member of Rosenfeld Media's "experts" group and writes about whatever's on his mind at aaron-gustafson.com.

CONTENTS

FOREWORD

I remember well when I got my hands on a copy of the first edition of *Adaptive Web Design*. I knew it would be good, but I didn't expect to be quite so blown away after just one chapter. In that first chapter, Aaron managed to perfectly crystallize what I had been struggling to articulate for years on the true meaning of progressive enhancement.

In hindsight, I shouldn't have been so surprised. Aaron is a multi-talented worker for the Web and has cultivated a deep knowledge of many areas—particularly accessibility. But his real talent lies not in his way with technology but in his way with people.

It's all too easy for us—web designers and developers—to get caught up in the details of technical implementations. If we're not careful, we can lose sight of the reasons why we're designing and developing on the Web in the first place. Aaron can take you on a deep dive into the minutiae of markup, the secrets of CSS, and the jargon of JavaScript, while at the same time reminding you of why any of it matters: the people who will be accessing your work.

I suspect that Aaron struggles to come up with a title to describe what he does. Developer? Evangelist? Author? All those terms describe parts Aaron's work, but they all fall short. I think the title that best describes Aaron Gustafson is…teacher.

Good teachers can work magic. They impart knowledge while weaving an entertaining tale at the same time. That's exactly what Aaron does with this book.

You're in for a treat. You're about to read a story that is as instructional as it is engrossing.

Take it away, teacher…

Jeremy Keith, Clearleft
August 2015

INTRODUCTION

Most web design books are filled with great techniques and examples that you can pick up and use right away. They're often filled with reams of documentation on which HTML tags to use in which situation and what each and every CSS property does. And most include some sort of sample project or projects for you to work along with in order to see how the code examples come together.

This is not that kind of book. This is a philosophy book about designing for the ever-changing, ever-evolving Web.

There are thousands of technique books out there for you to buy and hundreds of thousands of technique-based articles for you to read. Many of them are quite good. Sadly, however, most of them have a shelf life measured in months.

Technologies…browsers…toolsets…they're constantly changing. I struggle to keep up and often find myself overwhelmed, adrift on a churning sea of far too many options and ways I *could* be building websites. When I'm being tossed hither and thither by the waves, I affix my gaze on the one thing that helps me get my bearings and make sense of what's happening: the philosophy of progressive enhancement.

This philosophy—which is the heart and soul of an adaptive approach to web design—grounds me and helps me put any new technology, technique, or idea in perspective. Furthermore, it makes my sites more robust and capable of reaching more users with fewer headaches. It has made me a better web designer, and I know it can do the same for you.

"Anyone who slaps a 'this page is best viewed with Browser X' label on a Web page appears to be yearning for the bad old days, before the Web, when you had very little chance of reading a document written on another computer, another word processor, or another network."

—TIM BERNERS LEE

CHAPTER 1:
DESIGNING EXPERIENCES FOR PEOPLE

The one constant on the Web is change. There's always a new design fad; a new darling language, framework, or tool; a shiny new device to view it on; or new ideas of what it means to be "on the Web."

It's exceptionally difficult to wrap your head around an industry that is constantly in flux. It makes my head hurt, and if you've been working on the web for a while, I suspect you might feel the same.

Having worked on the Web for nearly two decades, I've seen the cycle play out over and over. Java applets, Shockwave, Flash, Prototype, jQuery, 960gs, Bootstrap, Angular, React…. Technologies come and go, but the Web remains. Screens went from tiny to huge and then back to tiny again, but the Web remains. Walled gardens were built and then torn asunder to make way for "app" stores and (yes) more walled gardens, but the Web remains.

The Web remains because it is not a fixed screen size. The Web remains because it is not a specific device. The Web doesn't need to be installed. The Web is inherently resilient and infinitely malleable. The Web has the capacity to go anywhere, do anything, and reach anyone.

SMART CODE, DUMB PHONES

In early 2012, my company began working with a client who was struggling with the security of their mobile apps. They had numerous native apps that all followed the common convention of using a web service to authenticate users. They are a very security-conscious organization, and this setup was creating a bottleneck in deploying new security features. To roll out a new security feature to their users (for example, a security question like "What was the name of your first school?"), they had to go through an excruciatingly long, arduous, multistep process:

1. Implement the new security feature.
2. Expose it via the web service.
3. Update each app to use the new web service (which might include user interface changes, and so on).
4. Submit each app for approval.
5. Hope their users downloaded the new version of the app.

They brought us in to reimagine the authentication flow as a web-based process that would launch inside an app—they had separate iPhone, iPad, and Android apps—and handle letting the app know whether and when the user had successfully logged in. This approach meant they could roll out new security features immediately because the apps and the authentication flow would be loosely coupled. Letting users sign in through a web page within the native app would be a huge win for everyone involved.

Despite that the project was aimed at handling authentication for mobile apps on three specific platforms, we built the web pages without getting hung up on technology or screen sizes. Instead, we focused on the purpose of every interface component and every screen. The layouts were responsive from tiny screens all the way up to large ones, and we implemented HTML5 and JavaScript in completely unobtrusive ways. We wanted to take advantage of cool new things (such as native form validation) while still keeping the file sizes small and ensuring the pages would function in the absence of either technology.

A few months after completing the project, our client came back to us with a second project: They wanted to roll out the authentication flow to their "m-dot" users (people who visited their mobile-only website). They gave us a list of nearly 1,400 unique User Agent strings that had accessed the login screen over a two-day period and asked whether we could handle it. We parsed the list[1] and were able to come up with a more manageable aggregate list of devices and device types to use in our testing. It was something like 25 devices that would cover roughly 97 percent of their 1,400 device spectrum. The last 3 percent was at the end of a long tail when it came to device usage, and we were comfortable assuming that fixing issues in the other 97 percent would likely cover them as well. That said, we were prepared to fix any additional issues when and if they cropped up.

Our budget for adding support for 1,400 new devices, including some heinous old browsers (for example, BlackBerry 4 and Openwave), was about one-third the budget of the original project that targeted only three.

Let that soak in for a second.

Now here's the kicker: When all was said and done, we came in at roughly *half* of our proposed budget, in terms of both actual hours billed and time to completion. It was awesome for us because we delivered ahead of schedule—which made us look good—and it earned our client contact major kudos from his bosses because he'd saved the company serious money on the project (which rarely happens in the corporate world).

It's worth noting that this accomplishment had nothing to do with our bug-squashing prowess or our speed—we just followed the philosophy of progressive enhancement.

---

1   With the help of a little script I cooked up: http://perma.cc/4EAE-Y9H5.

Progressive enhancement is a web design philosophy that embraces the very nature of the Web. It isn't about devices or browsers, and it's not about which version of HTML or CSS you can use. Using progressive enhancement means you craft experiences that serve your users by giving them access to content without technological restrictions.

It sounds pretty amazing, and anything *that* amazing must be a lot of work, right? Actually, it's not. Once you understand how progressive enhancement works, or more importantly *why* it works, you'll see it's quite simple. As we often say, progressive enhancement *just works*.

During a presentation at the South by Southwest Interactive Festival in 2003, Steve Champion of the Web Standards Project offered the term *progressive enhancement* to describe his vision for a new way to think about web design—starting with the content and building out from there. Once you understand what progressive enhancement is all about, it's hard to imagine approaching a project in any other way. It just makes sense. And yet, it took nearly a decade after the Web's creation for this approach to web design to be proposed, let alone embraced.[2]

WHEN THE WEB WAS YOUNG

In the beginning there was text:[3] the line mode browser.[4] It has a black screen with green text (**Figure 1.1**). You know, it was the kind of program hackers use in the movies.

---

2   We're still working on that one, which is the reason for this book.

3   Well, technically, in the beginning there was a graphical browser called WorldWideWeb (later Nexus), but it was available only on the NeXT operating system and never made it into general use.

4   Some of my friends and colleagues ventured back to CERN in 2013 to re-create the line mode browser using modern web technologies. They wrote about it, and you can try it out at http://perma.cc/2UYR-HVWP.

Figure 1.1 *The line mode browser as re-created in 2013.*

The line mode browser supported basic formatting such as indentation, centering, and the like, but that was about it. But it didn't matter. It was 1990. The Web was an infant and was all about publishing and reading text-based content, so it didn't need to look pretty.

By the time I got online five years later, things were a bit different. The National Center for Supercomputing Application's Mosaic had brought the graphical side of the Web to the masses two years earlier, and Netscape's Navigator was already a year old.[5]

But my experience of the Web in 1995 was not graphical. I was attending New College in Sarasota, Florida, and had to dial in to the campus's server in order to access the Internet. It was all done over the command line, and I saw my first website—sony.com—in stark black and white (**Figure 1.2**).

I thought to myself *This web thing is bullshit!* and quickly disconnected my modem in disgust.

5   Microsoft's Internet Explorer had just been born.

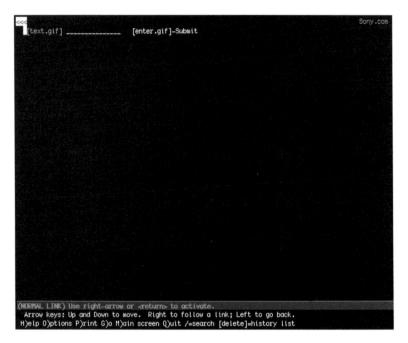

Figure 1.2 *My best approximation of what I saw the first time I used Lynx to access sony.com: a black screen with white text saying nothing.*

You know what? I was right: That experience was bullshit! Here was a website whose purpose was to disseminate information about Sony products and musicians and it had—effectively—no content. In other words, its purpose was lost.

How did this happen? Well, the folks who designed that version of sony.com had used images instead of actual page content. All the page text was rendered in JPEGs and GIFs. When they assembled the images onto the page, they failed to author alt text that provided access to that content. Anyone who couldn't partake of what I'm sure was the pinnacle of mid–1990s web design was pretty much screwed.

And so there I was, taking my first tentative steps onto the Web and I was denied access to a site because the technology I was using to access it was not advanced enough. I felt like the short kid at the amusement park, feigning disinterest in the Tilt-a-Whirl because I was the only one of my friends who was too small to ride it.

And just like my childhood height, my browser choice was not something I had control over. I couldn't have just downloaded Mosaic or bought a copy of Netscape at my local Babbage's and been on my merry way. Our school's server didn't support Point-to-Point Protocol (PPP) at the time, so I could browse only on the command line via Lynx.

That experience colored my perception of the Web and has stuck with me ever since, guiding my decisions as a web designer. I always think about my experience and the lack of accessibility the Web—well, sony.com specifically—had for me at the time. It sucked. I never want to make someone else feel like that.

TECHNOLOGY VS. EXPERIENCE

When the Web was young, the technologies we used to create experiences for it were rapidly evolving. HTML was not standardized like it is today, and Microsoft and Netscape were taking turns adding new elements and behaviors in a seemingly eternal game of one-upmanship. We also had things like Java applets,[6] RealMedia, Shockwave, Flash, and a host of other proprietary technologies that served only to complicate the page construction process and heaped additional requirements on our users.

---

6   Did you ever use one to make your content look like it was reflected in a pool of water? That was so cool!

As an industry, we adopted the engineering concept of *graceful degradation*, which ensures a system can continue to work with a reduced service level even when part of it is unavailable or destroyed. In other words, it's a philosophy meant to avoid catastrophe. In practice on the Web, this meant we assumed older browsers, or those without the necessary plug-ins, would get a poor experience. We rarely made the time to test in these scenarios, so we erected signs for our users:

This page works best in Internet Explorer.

This page looks best in Netscape.

You need Flash to use our website.

Keep out ye undesirables!

The graceful degradation philosophy amounted to giving the latest and greatest browsers the experience of a full-course meal, while tossing a few scraps to the sad folk unfortunate enough to be using an older or less-capable browser.

And when we really didn't feel like testing in a browser, we'd just read the User Agent string on the server and erect a roadblock (**Figure 1.3**).[7] After all, we told ourselves, if we stop the user before they experience an error, we're avoiding delivering a bad experience.

But is no experience better than a less than ideal experience? I don't think so.

---

7   Of course, few of us even did that well. A lot of User Agent sniffing (as it's called) is poorly done and results in false positives. It's been the driving factor for the "evolution" of the User Agent string. Nicholas Zakas wrote a brilliant piece chronicling that: http://perma.cc/BR7M-JEDH.

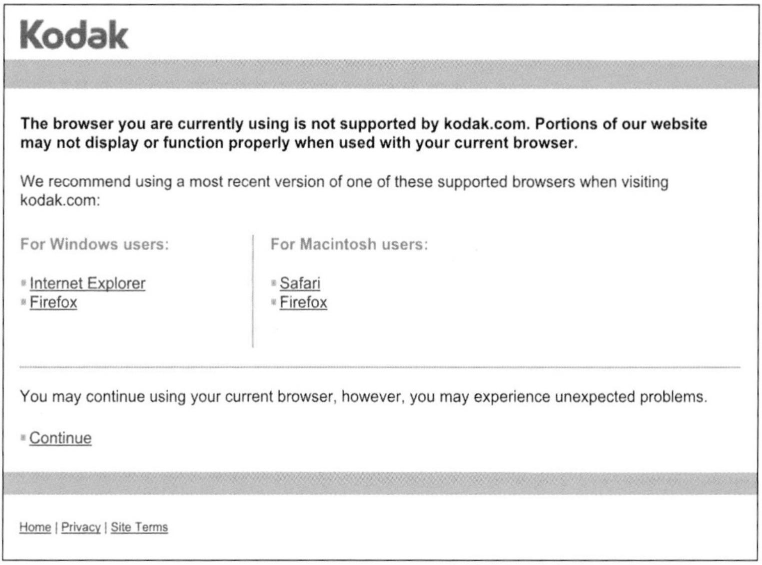

Figure 1.3 *An example roadblock page from Kodak.*

Lessons Learned at the Bleeding Edge

Some time ago I worked on a Chrome app for WikiHow.[8] As a Chrome app and a showpiece for the then-new Chrome Web Store, our client wanted it to have fancy CSS3 animations and transitions, web fonts, a WebSQL database, offline support, and lots of other "HTML5" bells and whistles. And, as our target was a single browser, we relented when asked to go the single-page app route. The app was built to degrade gracefully (it blocked non-WebKit browsers), but it was not progressively enhanced.

Skip ahead about a year and our client returned, asking us to add support for Firefox and Internet Explorer (IE) 9+. Oh boy.

---

8   http://perma.cc/5KE9-GK88.

Having built the site purely for WebKit, it was a bit of a challenge. In addition to implementation differences with the experimental CSS features, we also had to deal with the DOM (document object model) and JavaScript API (application programming interface) variance among the browsers. But the single biggest issue we ran into was the lack of WebSQL support in Firefox and IE.

You see, in the intervening year, WebSQL had been abandoned at the W3C (World Wide Web Consortium)—the organization that oversees most web standards—because of pushback (primarily from Mozilla and Microsoft). It was not available in either Firefox or IE, nor would it ever be. IndexedDB, the new replacement for WebSQL, had yet to be implemented in any production browser. So we ended up writing a wrapper on top of `localStorage` that looked a lot like SQL. Thankfully, that allowed us to avoid rewriting the bulk of the app. Incidentally, it also made the app a lot faster.

The total cost of the new compatibility project was around 40 percent of the budget to build the app the first time around. Without access to an alternate timeline, I can't be certain, but my experience tells me it would have added less than 40 percent to the original project had we been given the leeway to build it using progressive enhancement. Plus, the end result would have been even better because it would have been able to function without JavaScript.

Based on conversations I've had with other designers, the 40 percent number seems pretty accurate—possibly even a bit low. I remember one conversation several years ago about Google Maps. When the team originally built Maps—in all of its Ajax-y glory—they didn't make it accessible, and it required JavaScript. According to the source of this anecdote (who I have long forgotten), it took them almost twice as long to retrofit Maps as it would have taken had they built it from the ground up following progressive enhancement. As it's purely anecdotal, you should take that with a grain of salt, but it's food for thought.

Now consider this story in light of the one I shared earlier. Given the choice between a 40 percent budget increase to add support for 2 browsers and a 15 percent increase to add 1,400 browsers, I know which option I'd choose. Progressive enhancement does require a bit more thoughtful consideration up front. But the extra time required diminishes with practice, *and* the philosophy pays huge dividends in the long run. More reach, less overhead, fewer headaches.

Progressive enhancement trounces graceful degradation when it comes to reaching more browsers, devices, and (ultimately) users for less money (and fewer headaches). But how?

For starters, progressive enhancement recognizes that experience is a continuum.

YOU CAN'T PLEASE EVERYONE

Providing a pixel-perfect, wholly identical experience for each and every human being who tries to access your site would be impossible. There are simply far too many factors to consider.

On the technical side of things, you've got screen size, display density, CPU (central processing unit) speed, amount of RAM (random-access memory), sensor availability, feature availability, interface methods…*breathe*…operating system, operating system version, browser, browser version, plug-ins, plug-in versions, network speed, network latency, network congestion, firewalls, proxies, routers, and probably a dozen other factors my mind is incapable of plucking from the whirlwind of technological considerations.

And that doesn't even take into account your users' experiences interacting with your work.

When it comes to people, you have to consider literacy level, reading level, amount of domain knowledge, cognitive impairments such as learning disabilities and dyslexia, attention deficit issues, environmental distractions, vision impairment, hearing impairment, motor impairment, how much they understand how to use their device, how much they understand how to use their browser, how well-versed in common web conventions they are, and a ton of other "human factors."

Every person is different, and everyone comes to the Web with their own set of special needs. Some needs develop over time and persist—blindness, for example. Others are transient, such as breaking your mousing arm. Still others are purely situational and dependent on the device you are using at the time and its technical capabilities or constraints.

Trying to devise one monolithic experience for each and every person to have in every context that considers every factor would be impossible. Given unlimited time and budget, you could probably make it happen, but how often do you get to work under those conditions?[9] Designing for a monolithic experience is a form of arrogance—it assumes you will always know your users' context and what's best for them. In reality, you often know far less than you think you do.

And yet, Sir Tim Berners Lee—the guy who invented the World Wide Web—had a vision for a Web that was portable, capable of going anywhere.[10] Was he delusional?

SUPPORT THE PAST, OPTIMIZE FOR THE FUTURE

Back in middle school, I wrote every paper in Word for MS-DOS. It was a piece of software that did one thing really well: It allowed the user to focus on writing.[11] You didn't have a whole lot of options for formatting text, but it did what it needed to do, and it did it with aplomb.

9　If you do, in fact, get to work under these conditions, please let me know if you're hiring.

10　You can read his proposal here: http://perma.cc/H8HW-DACS.

11　In many ways, iA Writer—which I am using to write these very words—reminds me a lot of it.

More than two decades later, it's next to impossible for me to read the DOC files Word created for me. As an application, Word long abandoned support for reading and editing that generation of the DOC format.

Now I'm not saying that the stuff I wrote in middle school is really worth reading today (I'm sure it's not), but I am only one of millions of people who authored content in Word for DOS. That content is largely lost to history because the format evolved in a way that made newer versions of Word incapable of reading those older files.

And that's just one piece of software. We see these sort of "breaking changes" all the time in software, even on the Web. The popular JavaScript framework Angular changed so much between its 1.0 and 2.0 versions that developers had to rewrite their apps almost entirely to take advantage of its new features.

This is a huge challenge for archivists because even if they manage to hang on to a copy of the programs that originally authored these files, they also need to maintain machines capable of running the software (which is equally challenging).

When he conceived of the World Wide Web, Sir Tim Berners Lee wanted to avoid this problem. He wanted content on the Web to be robust and future-proof, so he made that a guiding principle of the web's *lingua franca*, HTML. To wit, the HTML 2.0 spec says this:[12]

> *To facilitate experimentation and interoperability between implementations of various versions of HTML, the installed base of HTML user agents supports a superset of the HTML 2.0 language by reducing it to HTML 2.0: markup in the form of a start-tag or end-tag, whose generic identifier is not declared is mapped to nothing during tokenization. Undeclared attributes are treated similarly. The entire attribute specification of an unknown attribute (i.e., the unknown attribute and its value, if any) should be ignored.*

12 http://perma.cc/H8HW-DACS

In other words, browsers are instructed to ignore what they don't understand. This is fault tolerance (another carry-over term from the world of engineering), and it's central to the design of HTML as a language and CSS as well.[13]

Both languages were designed to be "forward compatible," meaning everything you write today will work tomorrow and next year and in ten years. These languages were designed to evolve over time. By ignoring anything they don't understand, browsers give these languages room to grow and adapt without ever reaching a point where the content they encapsulate and style would no longer be readable or run the risk of causing a browser to crash.

Fault tolerance makes it possible to browse an HTML5-driven website in Lynx and allows you to experiment with CSS3 features without worrying about breaking Internet Explorer 6. Understanding fault tolerance is the key to understanding progressive enhancement. Fault tolerance is the reason progressive enhancement works and makes it possible to ensure all content delivered on the Web is accessible and available to everyone.

Maintaining Your Sanity

Trying to give everyone the same experience across the myriad device and browser combinations, especially considering the variety of human factors that affect how they interact with a page, would be a fool's errand. It's important to pick your battles. Web developer Brad Frost beautifully couched this approach as "support vs. optimization."

> Unless you want to hole yourself up in a cabin for the foreseeable future, you're not going to be able to optimize your web experience for every single browser. What I'm really asking for here is consideration.

13 http://perma.cc/MW47-P99F

You don't have to treat these browsers as equals to iOS and Android and no one is recommending that we have to serve up a crappy WAP site to the best smartphones on the market. It's just about being more considerate and giving these people who want to interact with your site a functional experience. That requires removing comfortable assumptions about support and accounting for different use cases. There are ways to support lesser platforms while still optimizing for the best of the best.[14]

By following this approach, you enable your content to go as far as possible, unencumbered by the requirements of some particular technology or capability. You can do this rather easily by focusing on the content and building up the experience, layer by layer, because the browser and device can adequately support that experience.

Progressive enhancement isn't about browsers or devices or technologies. It's about crafting experiences that serve your users by giving them access to content without technological restrictions. Progressive enhancement doesn't require that you provide the same experience to every user, nor does it preclude you from using the latest and greatest technologies; it simply asks that you honor your site's purpose and respect your users by applying technologies in an intelligent way, layer upon layer, to craft an amazing experience.

Browsers, devices, and technologies will come and go. Marrying progressive enhancement with your desire to be innovative and do incredible things is entirely possible—as long as you're smart about your choices and don't allow yourself to be so distracted by the shiny and new that you lose sight of your site's purpose or your users' needs.

---

14 http://perma.cc/D9ZP-H953

SERVING MORE FOR LESS

Of course, there are many folks who consider progressive enhancement—especially insofar as creating a non-JavaScript experience goes—a total waste of time. Take this comment a reader left on web developer Tim Kadlec's blog post "Crippling the Web:"[15]

> *This is all fine and dandy, but not very real world. A cost-benefit analysis has to happen—what does that next user/visitor cost, and more importantly earn you? This idealistic approach would leave most broke if they had to consider "every user" when building a site. That's why clothes come in small, medium, large, and extra-large. Most of us have to buy them that way because not everyone can afford a tailor made suit, much less an entire wardrobe. Your approach only works for those who can see the return.*

Tim's response was dead-on:

> *I think that's where the difference between 'support' and 'optimization' comes into play. I'm certainly not saying to go out and buy every device under the sun, test on them, make sure things look and behave the same. You don't necessarily have to optimize for all these different devices and scenarios (that's where the cost-benefit analysis has to come in), but it's often not very time consuming to at least support them on some level.*

> *Progressive enhancement can get you a long way towards accomplishing that goal. Sometimes it's as simple as doing something like 'cutting the mustard' to exclude older devices and browsers that might choke on advanced JS from having to try and deal with that. The experience isn't the same, but if you've used progressive enhancement to make sure the markup is solid and not reliant on the JavaScript, it's at least something that is usable for them.*

---

15 http://perma.cc/AR56-T6GD

You can't test every scenario, every browser, and every device. There just aren't enough hours in the day even if someone was willing to spend the money on doing it—and guess what, they aren't. You need to balance your desired reach with your realistic resources.

This is why progressive enhancement is so helpful. You can provide a baseline experience that anyone can use and then look for ways to improve it on the browsers and devices that are part of your test matrix.

As an added bonus, you'll be able to reach new devices as they roll out with little to no extra effort. Case in point: The TechCrunch redesign of 2013 did not prioritize the browsing experience on a tiny screen, but they allowed for it; as a result, the site looks and works just as well on a smart watch (**Figure 1.4**) as it does on a phone or a desktop screen.

Progressive enhancement is inherently *future friendly.*[16]

Figure 1.4 *TechCrunch viewed on an Android Wear device.*

UNIVERSAL ACCESSIBILITY

Sir Tim's vision for the Web was that content could be created once and accessed from anywhere. Disparate but related pieces of "hypermedia"[17] scattered across the globe could be connected to one another via links. Moreover, they would be retrievable by anyone on any device capable of reading HTML. For free.

Ultimately, Sir Tim's vision is about accessibility.

For a great many of us, ensuring our websites are accessible is an afterthought. We talk a good game when it comes to "user centered" this or that but often treat the word *accessibility* as a synonym for "screen reader."

Sure, people with visual impairments often use a screen reader to consume content. But they might also use a braille touch feedback device or a braille printer. They probably also use a keyboard. Or they may use a touchscreen in concert with audio cues. Or they may even use a camera to allow them to "read" content via optical character recognition (OCR) and text-to-speech. And yes, visual impairment affects a decent percentage of the populace (especially as we age, which we all do), but it is only part of the "accessibility" puzzle.

We all benefit when designers consider accessibility. We all have special needs. "Accessibility" is about recognizing that fact and taking steps to address them.

People consume content and use interfaces in many different ways, some similar and some quite dissimilar to how you do it. Designing for universal accessibility means not imposing a certain world view—yours, your boss's, or your client's—on how or where someone is going to access your website, giving your users ultimate control on how they choose to consume your content.

The dimensions of interactive elements—links, buttons, and so on—and their proximity to one another is an important factor in

---

17 Sir Tim used the term *hypermedia* because he knew the Web would need to contain more than just text.

ensuring an interface actually registers your intent. Have you ever injured your dominant arm and had to mouse with your other one? It's frustrating, especially when links are small or buttons are too close together. Visual design is an accessibility concern.

The color contrast between text and the background is an important factor in ensuring content remains readable in different lighting situations. Some websites are nearly impossible to read on your phone while outside on a sunny day or when you've turned down the screen brightness to sip that last 5 percent of your battery life. Color choice is an accessibility concern.

The language you use on your sites and in your interfaces directly affects how easy it is for your users to understand what you do, the products you're offering, and why it matters. It also affects how you make your users feel about themselves, their experience, and your company. Terms of service are a perfect example of this: No one reads them because they are alienating and unfriendly.[18] Language is an accessibility concern.

The size of your web pages and their associated assets has a direct effect on how long your pages take to download, how much it costs your customers to access them, and (sometimes) even whether the content can be reached. One time I unwittingly played 30 minutes of a high-definition video while tethered to my phone, traveling abroad, thanks to YouTube's auto-play "feature."[19] It cost me about $30. Bandwidth use and performance are accessibility concerns.

I could keep going, but I'm sure you get the point.

To me, accessibility is ultimately about ensuring people have equal opportunity to access your content while simultaneously recognizing that we all have special needs—physical limitations, bandwidth limitations, device limitations—that may require each of us to have different experiences of the same web page.

---

18 Except Medium's; they're awesome! See http://perma.cc/EDS6-5VZC.

19 http://perma.cc/CS5G-S72K

When I load a website on my phone, for example, I am visually limited by my screen resolution (especially if I am using a browser that encourages zooming), and I am limited in my ability to interact with buttons and links because I am browsing with my fingertips, which are far larger and less precise than a mouse cursor. On a touchscreen, I may need the experience to be slightly different, but I still need to be able to do whatever it is I came to the page to do. I need *an experience*, but moreover, I need *the appropriate experience*.

Experience doesn't need to be one hulking, monolithic ideal. It can be different for different people. That may be hard to wrap your head around at times, but embracing it will help you reach more people with fewer headaches.

Experience can—and should—be crafted as a continuum. Progressive enhancement *embraces* that continuum.

THINKING IN LAYERS

One analogy I like to use for progressive enhancement are Peanut M&M's (**Figure 1.5**). At the center of each Peanut M&M's candy is, well, the peanut. The peanut itself is a rich source of protein and fat—a great food that everyone can enjoy (except those with an allergy, of course). In a similar sense, the content of your website should be able to be enjoyed without embellishment.

Figure 1.5 *A confectionary continuum from peanut to Peanut M&M's.*

Slather that peanut with some chocolate and you create a mouth-watering treat that, like the peanut, also tastes great. So too, content beautifully organized and arranged using CSS is often easier to understand and certainly more fun to consume.

By coating your nutty confection with a sugary candy shell, the experience of this treat is improved yet again. In a similar sense, you can cap off your beautiful designs with engaging JavaScript-driven interactions that ease your user's movement through the content or bring it to life in unique and entertaining ways.

This is, of course, an oversimplification of progressive enhancement, but it gives you a general sense of how it works. Technologies applied as layers can create different experiences, each one equally valid (and tasty). And at the core of it all is the nut: great content.

Progressive enhancement asks you to begin with the core experience that is universally accessible and improve that experience when you can. Benjamin Hoh eloquently put it this way: [20]

> [Progressive enhancement] keeps the design open to possibilities of sexiness in opportune contexts, rather than starting with a 'whole' experience that must be compromised.

More often than not, experience begins with content. Clear, well-written, and well-organized content provides solid footing for any web project. It's important to ensure that content is universally available too, which means it needs to be addressable via HTTP.[21]

To enhance the meaning of your content, to make it more expressive, you use markup. Every element has a purpose. Some elevate the importance of a word or phrase, others clarify the role a selection of content is playing in the interface, and still others aggregate collections of elements into related sections of a document. Markup gives more meaning to your content.

---

20 http://perma.cc/MZK5-5AL9

21 As web developer Tantek Çelik puts it, "If it's not curlable, it's not on the Web." See http://perma.cc/6Y8C-AZB6.

Visual design is a means of establishing hierarchy on a page. Contrast, repetition, proximity, and alignment help to guide users through your content quickly and easily. Visual design also helps you reinforce your brand and provide the most appropriate reading experience given the amount of screen real estate available to you.

You can use interaction as a means of reducing the friction of an interface. Hiding content until it is needed, providing real-time feedback based on user input, and enabling your users to accomplish more on a single page without constant page refreshes go a long way in humanizing an interface. They help your users be more productive and, when done well, can even make your creations delightful to use.

These levels, when stacked upon one another, create an experience that grows richer with every step, but they are by no means the only experiences that will be had by a user. In fact, they are simply identifiable milestones on the path from the most basic experience to the most exceptional one (**Figure 1.6**). A user's actual experience may vary at one or more points along the path and that's all right; as long as you keep progressive enhancement in mind, your customers will be well served.

A website built following the philosophy of progressive enhancement will be usable by anyone on any device, using any browser. A user on a text-based browser like Lynx won't necessarily have the same experience as a user surfing with the latest version of Chrome, but the key is that the user will have a positive experience rather than no experience at all. The content of the website will be available, albeit with fewer bells and whistles.

In many ways, progressive enhancement is a Zen approach to web design: Control what you can up until the point at which you must relinquish control and let go.

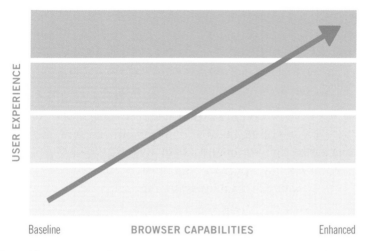

Figure 1.6 *Progressive enhancement visualized: the user experience gets better as opportunity allows.*

THIS IS A PHILOSOPHY

Progressive enhancement is a philosophy that pays huge dividends in terms of time, cost, and reach. It reminds you to embrace the Web's inherent "webbiness" and helps you reach your users where they are, in the most appropriate way possible.

It all begins with embracing the concept of experience as a continuum. In the following chapters, you'll explore what that means and how to integrate the progressive enhancement philosophy into your web design process.

"Content precedes design. Design in the absence of content is not design, it's decoration."

—JEFFREY ZELDMAN

CHAPTER 2:
CONTENT IS THE FOUNDATION

Over the 2011 holidays, Facebook users uploaded photos like crazy. In just a few days, Facebook processed more photo uploads than are contained in the entirety of Flickr. Seriously, that's a lot of photos.

One unintended consequence of this deluge of photo uploads was a significant uptick in people asking Facebook to remove specific ones. Facebook received millions of these "photo reports," but they made no sense: moms holding babies reported for harassment, pictures of puppies reported for hate speech, and so on. Roughly 97 percent of these photo reports were dramatically miscategorized.

Facebook's engineers reached out to some of the users who had reported these photos to get a bit more background regarding their submissions. At the time Facebook's photo-reporting interface provided a list of reasons users could choose from if they wanted a photo removed, but, as Facebook soon discovered, many of the reports were made because users didn't want the photo posted for reasons other than those provided. In some cases, it was because they didn't like how they looked in the photo. In others, it was because the photo was of an ex-partner or even a beloved pet they'd shared with an ex-boyfriend or ex-girlfriend.

The existing photo-reporting tool had not done a good job of accounting for these more personal reasons for wanting a photo removed, so the Facebook engineers went to work. They added a step that asked, "How does this photo make you feel?" The options were simple.

- Embarrassing
- Upsetting
- Saddening
- Bad photo
- Other

The Other option also provided a free-response text field to fill in.

With this system in place, Facebook engineers found that 50 percent of reporters who answered the new question chose one of the provided options. That was pretty helpful, but there was still a problem: 34 percent of the respondents who chose Other were writing "It's embarrassing" in the blank rather than choosing the Embarrassing option already provided.

What the Facebook team realized was that people were not identifying with the Embarrassing option (or may have even thought it was referring to them rather than assuming the implied "It's"). A subtle shift in language was needed, so they changed the label to "Please describe the photo," and they updated the options to mirror how people actually talk.

- It's embarrassing
- It's a bad photo of me
- It makes me sad

With this subtle change, they were able to increase the percentage of photo reporters who chose one of the options provided to a whopping 78 percent.[1]

---

1   This story appeared in RadioLab's episode "The Trust Engineers." You can listen to it at http://perma.cc/WZJ7-AK9X.

Words matter. Even in something as simple and banal as a form, the words you choose set the tone for your users' experiences and often have an effect on what they do, or fail to do.

The text of your interfaces—especially form labels and responses—is just one small part of the content picture. There are many other types of content, such as product descriptions, marketing copy, legal statements, photography, illustrations, visualizations, video, audio, and more. However, when we think about "content," we often equate it with "copy." This is no doubt a carry-over from the marketing world where "copywriters" were tasked with authoring the text for an advertisement or campaign.

"Content," as a word, kinda sucks. It feels dry, mechanical, boring, tedious. It's generic and nonspecific. No one ever jumped out of bed in the morning shouting "Today I'm going to make content!" In fact, it fits perfectly as a blanket term for that lifeless corporate communications drivel we endure on a day-to-day basis.

And yet, "content" is where experience begins. We often lose sight of that.

The role of the traditional copywriter was to collaborate with an art director on the message and purpose of a campaign. How should it make someone feel? What actions should it prompt them to take? Copywriters created a conversation with their audience that was so much larger than the words they employed.

Words, as they say, are cheap. Without a message, a purpose, words become weak. We can (and often do) author page upon page of flowery prose without saying anything. To write effective copy, it's important to know what the words need to be doing. To employ progressive enhancement, it's crucial to understand the role that content plays—it's the foundation upon which experiences are built.

AVOID ZOMBIE COPY

At the center of every interface is a conversation. You engage your users directly in an effort to inform them, entertain them, or persuade them to act in a particular way. How this conversation goes will directly affect the experience your users have.

When you speak to a friend or even a stranger, you speak with enthusiasm, interest, and…well…like a human. `YOU DO NOT RESPOND TO YOUR HUMAN COMPANION'S QUERIES WITH A SERIES OF WORDS THAT ARE OF A LIFELESS AND ROBOTIC NATURE.` And yet, that's the way scads of sites on the Web sound. Just because your content is managed in, delivered via, and displayed by a computer doesn't mean it needs to sound like it was written by one.

In her article "Attack of the Zombie Copy," content strategist Erin Kissane highlighted a real-world example of this.[2]

> *Incorporating our corporate culture into our business processes and customer needs, we continue to leverage our exceptional and effective work practices, improve operational effectiveness to meet business objectives and create win-win situations for our employees and shareholders.*

Wow. Now I'm not a violent man, but if someone said that to me at a cocktail party, I might have to slap them. Don't tell me you wouldn't.

We don't speak like that in person, so why should we speak like that online (or anywhere for that matter)? It's impossible to connect with content that reads like this. How do you have a conversation with a robot (or a zombie)?

---

2   http://perma.cc/2RMB-FS2W

Conversation is the basis for every user interaction. Don't believe me? Here are a few examples:

- **Home page**: You've just met someone and are explaining what you do (and, in some cases, why it matters). It goes best if you can find a way to relate what you do to something they've experienced.
- **Contact form**: You are trying to understand what someone needs in order to help them. Managing their expectations is key; let them know how long it may take you to get back to them.
- **Product page**: You are explaining what this object or service is, what it does, and how it will benefit them. If you know the type of person you'll be having this conversation with ahead of time, you'd plan ahead so you're ready to answer their questions quickly and easily.
- **Status update**: You're there to help someone open up… and then you shut up and listen (and mine their data for marketing purposes).

When you approach interfaces as conversations, it humanizes the interactions and improves your users' experiences. It also helps you focus on the important stuff so you don't get caught up in the act of writing.

DESIGN MEANINGFUL CONTENT

Diving into etymology for a moment here, *design* comes from the Latin *designare*, meaning "to mark out or indicate." The purpose of design is not to make something pretty; it's to clarify.

Words are powerful. They can obscure just as easily as they can illuminate. When you author content, you need to consider not only what you write but how you write it. Are you being unnecessarily vague? Are you using too much jargon or assuming too much domain-specific knowledge from your readers? Are you writing to the appropriate reading level? Are you being respectful? Are you writing in a way that connects your readers with your products or your brand? *Is your content serving a purpose?*

Asking these questions may be second nature to you, but I've encountered countless projects where content was clearly an afterthought, something that was stubbed out with nonsensical Latin text and gray boxes. We often take these shortcuts in our eagerness to tuck into "design" as quickly as possible, but that very decision undermines what it means to be a designer in the first place.

Content strategist Liam King was dead-on when he said this:

> *The problem with Lorem Ipsum is it conveniently fills the available space like an expanding gas. Unfortunately, it is inert, meaningless and lacks context, revealing very little about the relationship between the design and the content.*[3]

We often use fake text—a.k.a. Lorem Ipsum—as a tool to help us make some progress on designing an interface while we are waiting for "final, approved copy" (as though such a thing exists). We're not etching this stuff in marble tablets, folks—we're writing software. Start by writing the kind of copy you want to read. You can always change things later.[4]

An added bonus of authoring real copy early is that even if you forget to replace it, you end up with something that's halfway decent rather than something horribly embarrassing (**Figure 2.1**).[5]

---

3   http://perma.cc/QFB7-ZKHF

4   Lorem Ipsum isn't always the worst thing in the world. If you find that real copy is a distraction in design review meetings, for instance—Bob keeps nitpicking the copywriting—you can always sub in Lorem Ipsum for that specific context. Content strategist Karen MacGrane discusses this and other uses for Lorem Ipsum at http://perma.cc/N9UR-PHDJ.

5   Product designer Rian van der Merwe has amassed quite a collection of "placeholder" texts that have made it out into the wild: http://perma.cc/MT48-NQPH.

Figure 2.1 *Lorem Ipsum on a wine bottle as discovered by Rian van der Merwe.*

By focusing on how your interfaces read, you can gauge how well the copy you've written helps or hinders users to accomplish their goals. Words are the core of virtually every experience on the Web, and if you don't consider that from the beginning, no amount of breathtaking visual design or incredible JavaScript gymnastics are going to salvage it.

CRAFT THE CONVERSATION

Content strategist Stephanie Hay is a proponent of copy-driven interfaces and has seen great success with this approach. She begins collaboratively authoring real copy early in the process—even at kickoff![6]

To do so effectively, she offers the following guidelines:

1. Focus on writing actual content for the most sought-after content FIRST.

---

6   Stephanie Hay's template for kicking off new projects is publicly available at `http://perma.cc/X532-Q8LH`.

2. Ignore structure and flow—focus entirely on:
   • What is a realistic conversation we have with users on specific topics?
   • How can we clearly anticipate or answer their questions?
   • What's the end result of that conversation—a sign-up? A referral?
3. Create content that describes a realistic conversation you have with the target audience.

These guidelines are invaluable for keeping copy clear and focused. They also do wonders for clarifying the purpose of a project, which is all too easy to lose sight of in the rush to get it done and out the door.

A solid product or project strategy acknowledges the myriad moving pieces and looks for ways to connect them in support of the project's purpose. Without this orchestration, every facet of the project is left to chance and can cause the whole thing to fall apart. Copywriting is a powerful tool for tying it all together.

Another benefit of using copywriting in this way is that it forms a narrative but doesn't dictate design or interaction. It becomes a touchstone that each and every member of the team can reference to keep them mindful of the conversation they're having.

If the purpose of your site is to get a potential customer (let's call him Ben) to purchase a craft dog biscuit, your conversation with him might go a little something like this:

1. Explain what's in most dog biscuits. *Eeew!*
2. Talk about the dog-appropriate, natural ingredients in your dog biscuits. *Yum!*
3. Offer Ben a free sample pack or free shipping on a trial order. *Nice!*
4. Let Ben know that you believe so much in your biscuits that if his dog doesn't like them, you'll refund his order in full. *That's reassuring.*
5. If he tries the biscuits, you'll follow up a week after shipping to see how it's going. You'll offer him an easy way to start a subscription or a painless way to get a refund. *Wow, that's easy!*

6. If Ben goes for a subscription, you'll throw a few sample packs in there and ask him to share them with his friends. *Awesome! I'll pass these around at the dog park.*

While bare-bones—forgive the pun—this is a simple way to outline the experience you want Ben to have. It's also the perfect framework for fleshing out the real copy for your pages, emails, and so on, because you know what you want to say and what sort of reaction you are hoping to elicit from Ben. And you've even accounted for what happens if Ben is unhappy with the product, ensuring his experience of the company is always a positive one.

Mapping out user experience as a conversation can be invaluable for ensuring every decision you make in strategy, design, and production offers a positive contribution to that conversation. It isn't prescriptive about the way the page should be designed or what technology choices should be made. It does, however, make it clear that burying the "request a refund" button would be a no-no. Similarly, it helps you prioritize the content of your pages and informs you of what is crucial (and what's not).

Prepare for Problems

It's great when things go well, but what about when things go badly? As a user, there are few worse feelings than having a form you just filled out spit back to you because it contained errors.

Errors are one of those things you hope no one ever encounters, but someone always does. As users, they catch us off-guard and make us feel vulnerable and uneasy. As copywriters, it's your job to be there for your users to ease the tension, reassure them that it's not the end of the world, and help them quickly and easily remedy the issue.

Email marketing platform MailChimp does a fantastic job integrating this sort of thinking into its process. In fact, MailChimp's content director, Kate Kiefer Lee, created a whole site, Voice and

Tone,[7] that details how copywriters should be speaking to their customers in various situations, with a clear focus on their users' mental state and instructions on how to author copy that helps the situation rather than making it worse (**Figure 2.2**).

Figure 2.2 *MailChimp's Voice and Tone resource, covering how to notify a user of a system failure.*

For instance, when something goes wrong, the site acknowledges that the user is likely feeling confusion, stress, and possibly even anger. It offers what the user might be thinking—"What went wrong? I really need to get this campaign out."—and then offers some tips on how to author copy that will be helpful rather than harmful:

- Offer a solution or next step.
- Be straightforward. Explain what's going on right away.
- Be calm. Don't use exclamation points or alarming words like *alert* or *immediately*.
- Be serious. Don't joke around with people who are frustrated.

---

7   http://perma.cc/PAW2-LYCA. See also MailChimp's fantastic Style Guide: http://perma.cc/GQK6-79CM.

The guide even offers a good example that follows these guidelines: "We're experiencing a problem at one of our data centers. Our engineers are on the case and will have things back to normal shortly."

Simple. Direct. Clear. Conversational.

This level of care for their users shows them respect. It creates a reassuring experience for them, and consequently, MailChimp stands out as a company that cares about its customers.

It's also worth noting that putting together a guide like this helps you scale your content creation to more individual contributors as your project grows and your customer touchpoints become more diverse. It's a great way to keep everyone on the team speaking with a unified voice, further solidifying your brand's personality in the mind of your users.

PLAN FOR THE UNKNOWN

While the vast majority of web projects can use real content to drive a project, there are many project types (or portions of projects) where this is simply not feasible. Some projects need to be designed to handle a constant influx of new content, such as a blog, a news site, or your Twitter feed.

But even if you don't have all the content that will find a home on your site from the outset, all is not lost. You just need to think about the types of content you will need to support.

Thinking about the content you write in a systematic way can help ensure the words you author are assembled in a manner that best realizes their purpose. Designer Mark Boulton put it beautifully.[8]

> *You can create good experiences without knowing the content. What you can't do is create good experiences without knowing the structure. What is your content* made *from, not what your content* is. *An important distinction.*

---

8 http://perma.cc/5ZHY-GXBA

Content is hard. In my 20 years building websites, content has been the number-one factor that has put those projects at risk. But as Mark says, the content, while important, doesn't need to be complete. You don't need "final, approved copy" to begin designing, coding, or developing. What you need to know is what the content is, all the bits it comprises, and which of those bits are optional. This forms the basis of a site's information architecture.

If you are building a blog, for instance, you can't write all the copy before you launch the site; that would be absurd. What you can do, however, is take stock of the kinds of content you will be posting and use that to establish a consistent structure for each post.

For instance, you might know that every blog post will have a title and a body. But maybe every post needs a teaser sentence or two as well. That content could be used on an aggregation page (for example, the home page), or it might be used when the post is shared on a social network or found in search results.

Maybe you want all blog posts to have a unique image for use in the header, or maybe that's a "nice-to-have" feature that's optional.

If this blog is a solo undertaking, you may not need to capture the author, but if you might consider guest posts in the future, perhaps you should allow for that but make it optional. Tags, pull quotes, references, and more might be appropriate to some posts but not others.

Taken together, these bits form a blog post, but you don't need to know what every blog post that you will ever write is in order to design a blog template. You simply need to know what bits constitute a blog post and which of those are optional. It also helps to have a rough idea of how many words, images, videos, and so on, to expect in each.

You can repeat this process for each unique content type on the site, and it will give you a clear picture of what you are dealing with. All of this information can also be taken into account when designing the CMS (content management system) that powers the blog (**Figure 2.3**).

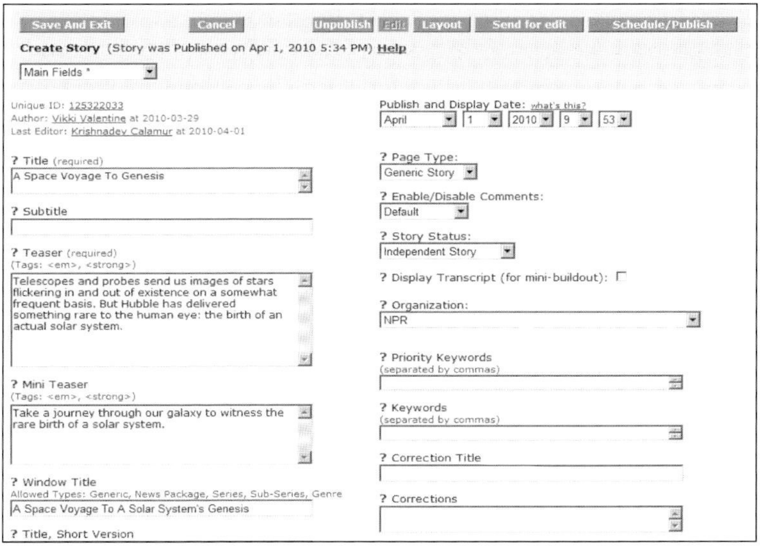

Figure 2.3 *NPR's CMS showing a handful of the component pieces of a story (from a presentation by Zach Brand of NPR, available at* `http://perma.cc/398N-5572`).

Thinking of content in this way creates the structure that is the fundamental first step in creating any experience. You need to know what Lego bricks you have in your pile before you can even hope to assemble them into something that makes any sense.

But I Don't Know the First Thing About Structured Content!

Thinking about structured content like this can be tough at first, so don't worry if it doesn't come naturally to you. If you find it challenging to think about it all in the abstract, find some examples of similar content that you can use as a reference.

If you are working on a blog or news site, you can go to a similar site and dissect one of its posts, teasing out the component pieces. You can compare different posts on the same blog and see whether some of the bits are optional. You can view the source of the page to unearth things such as teasers that might be hiding in `meta` tags. Then you can do it all over again for another site.

If you are working on an e-commerce site, you can view a competitor's site and perform the same sort of audit on its product listings. You can check the product page information against what you see for that same product in search results and on category landing pages. Are there multiple descriptions of varying lengths for different contexts? Are there abbreviated feature lists and full ones? Noting subtle differences like this helps you understand how your competitor is structuring things under the hood. Then you can go to another competitor and repeat the process.

Once you have the content structure nailed, it will be the roadmap for building out the CMS. And while you're waiting on real content to get entered into the system, you can use the representative content you found in your research (at least the bits you like) as the content that drives the experience. It's way better than Lorem Ipsum.

WRITE FOR REAL PEOPLE

In addition to helping you to stay true to your purpose, using the "content first" approach to designing experiences also ensures that your content is accessible to every potential user.

When I speak of accessibility, it's easy to get quickly overwhelmed by all the considerations—as I discussed in Chapter 1, everyone has special needs. It's daunting to even consider how to address a fraction of these many and varied concerns. This is when it helps to come back to thinking of experience as a continuum. That continuum needs to start somewhere, and it starts with your content.

When you craft content (or work with someone who does), think about how the interface reads. How straightforward is the writing? Is it lousy with jargon? Are you speaking to your audience the way they speak to you or to each other? Are you addressing your users as equals? Clear, well-written, and audience-appropriate prose is accessible to anyone. When you consider how your interfaces read, first you create a solid foundation on which to build a great experience.

CONSIDER CONTENT BEYOND COPY

When I discuss "content," I'm often speaking of the written word. But content isn't limited to copy. Photos, videos, audio files, PDFs, tables, interactive charts, iconography…those are all content too. They deserve as much consideration as the prose you author.

Pictures, sound, and video content can greatly enhance the experience of an interface. They can bring copy to life and, when done well, can provide clarity for your users that would be a struggle with words alone. And they can do so much more succinctly in the same way a single frame of HBO's *Game of Thrones* can convey as much information as a dozen pages of George R. R. Martin's prose.

But media can also be an unnecessary distraction. When you begin to consider the concrete experience of downloading a web page on a mobile device over a 3G or slower connection, the giant, beautiful, high-resolution imagery you loved so much becomes problematic. It's often the same when accessing content in an airport, train station, or hotel over wifi—it's never fast enough, and waiting for images to download can be a drag when you're rushing to catch your flight. There are also occasions where images themselves are not a problem from a download standpoint, but they cause the text content you're trying to read to break in odd ways on smaller screens, disrupting the reading experience.

Conduct a Cost-Benefit Analysis

When working with media, you need to ask the hard question: "Does this content actually add to the experience?" The answer doesn't need to be a binary "yes" or "no." It can be more nuanced than that. As with many factors that affect your decisions regarding how to build a website, *it depends*. It's important to weigh the pros and cons of including each photo, video, chart, or PDF in light of what you are trying to achieve on a given page.

How much time does a given image add to the download and rendering of the page? Will that time reduce the effectiveness of the page? Will it result in lost sales or leads? Or is the image so compelling that it will increase purchases or make a page more effective? Are the answers to those questions universal, or do they differ when the screen sizes do? What about over mobile networks?

As an example, consider the World News page of the *New York Times* (**Figure 2.4**). This page is brimming with teasers for full stories, each hoping to catch your eye. Our eyes are naturally drawn to contrasting elements on the page, so coupling an image with the text can increase that story's visibility amid a sea of competing prose.

Figure 2.4 The New York Times' *World News landing page. Note the numerous tiny thumbnails that don't add much to the story.*

Given the priority of stories on the page, these images could be beneficial, helping to guide users to the most important stories of the day. That's a UX win!

And yet, these images can be problematic too. Depending on the size of the image, a thumbnail could cause the text to flow oddly when viewed on a small screen. When the natural flow of content is interrupted, it makes the reading experience unpleasant and awkward. As an example of this, consider the *Guardian*'s website,[9] as shown in Opera Mobile on an HTC Wildfire (**Figure 2.5**). Sure, layout is something that the page designers should be thinking about, but that's not the only potential issue with these images.

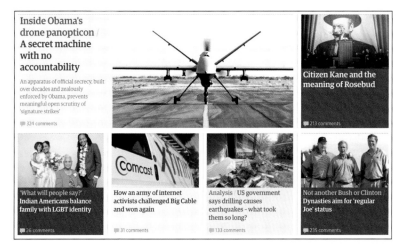

Figure 2.5 *Compare a section of the* Guardian *as rendered at "full size" on a large desktop screen in Chrome with an individual teaser as rendered by Opera Mobile on an HTC Wildfire at a resolution of 240×320. Note the text wrapping and awkward layout on the small screen.*

Consider page performance. Each of those images must be requested from the server and downloaded. On slower connections, that can significantly increase the time required to render the page. In the case of the *Guardian* example, the page weighs about 1.5MB and takes 1.6 seconds to begin rendering on Chrome over a 3G connection. It takes 27 seconds to fully load. Nearly half the requests from the browser are for images, and they also account for a third of the page weight.[10]

Performance and user experience are intrinsically linked. And while performance may seem like something the server admin should be concerned with, your decisions at the content level can limit your team's options when it comes to performance-tuning a site. You need to consider performance from the beginning of a project.

As web developer Tim Kadlec said, it all starts with the content.[11]

> *At first glance, it seems unlikely that content strategy would be a performance consideration. Frequently the people doing content strategy seem to be as far removed from the process of performance optimization as we could possibly imagine. But content decisions can have powerful, and long-lasting, impacts on performance.*

Performance matters to your users, even if it is (as Tim also says) "a lot like plumbing: No one talks about it until it's busted."[12]

Then there's the cost in terms of real money. On a metered connection, users are paying by the bit to download our content. Using Tim's insightful tool What Does My Site Cost?,[13] you can see that the *Guardian* home page would cost the average American about 11 cents to download on the least expensive mobile data plan. By

---

10 http://perma.cc/EB4J-P4QL

11 http://perma.cc/X7FN-ZY7G

12 http://perma.cc/X4US-HP2G

13 http://perma.cc/PAK9-QDDB

contrast, a user in Vanuatu will pay about 50 cents in U.S. dollars for the same content (more than 6 percent of their daily income).[14]

These may seem like technical challenges to solve, but content strategy dictates experience. Does it make sense to not have the images and have the large-screen usability suffer because you can't draw your users' eyes effectively? Or should you force your mobile users to suffer slow render times and costly downloads only to get images that don't add much to the experience?

The answer, as I've said, is *it depends*. Each situation is different, but when you are looking at your content, you need to be prepared to make a judgment call on whether a particular piece of content adds to the experience.

I will say that it is possible to have it both ways in certain circumstances. For instance, if you decide that thumbnails *are* valuable but not the most valuable content on the page, you could deem them "nice to have." In other words, you could deem them an enhancement. Once you make that call, there are technical means of having just the text content on small screens and having images on larger displays. I'll discuss this concept, called *lazy loading*, in Chapter 5.

All of this ignores the elephant in the room, of course: the actual monetary cost and time required to produce imagery, videos, and the like. Does the cost of licensing photographs—or of producing your own photoshoots and doing the follow-up editing and re-touching—outweigh any potential increase in sales (if you can even make the case that your photos will increase sales)? Video and animation can increase engagement, but they take time to storyboard, script, capture, and produce (particularly on an ongoing basis). That can be a significant time-suck and dramatically increase the cost of a project. Will you see a return on those investments?

---

14 http://perma.cc/Z445-6FBR

Avoid Trapping Content

When you are working with media—especially rich media such as interactive charts, videos, and the like—it can be quite easy to view the content of those media as pointless in any other form. This could not be further from the truth.

When you create an interactive chart, for example, it is the visualization of information. That visualization might be charting something specific such as sales data. That's information that could also be easily conveyed in a table.[15]

Sometimes, however, a literal translation from one medium to another is unnecessary. Take the graph Vanguard uses to highlight how much its customers save in fees (**Figure 2.6**). This graphic, though interactive, is simply an approximation and is not meant to be taken literally. The text paired with it does a great job of conveying the *spirit* of the graphic.

> We don't have any stockholders or outside owners to answer to. So we can run our funds at cost, and you get to keep more of your returns. On average, Vanguard mutual fund expense ratios are 82% less than the industry average.* Over time, that means more money can stay in your pocket.

Sometimes that's all you need. In other cases, that wouldn't be enough. For instance, consider a stock performance chart.

From a technical standpoint, it might make sense to store the content of the chart in an HTML table and convert it into a chart using JavaScript. Or it might make more sense to provide a link below the interactive chart to take users to a separate page containing the data tables. Depending on the situation, you may want to outline which is preferred as part of the content strategy, or it might be something that can be left up to the development team.

---

15   In fact, the data probably exists in some sort of database table (or maybe a few), which hints at another way it can be represented.

Figure 2.6 *This animated graph from Vanguard goes into detail about how much you stand to save by investing with the company, but the text above it perfectly conveys the spirit of the graphic. A video version is available at* http://perma.cc/L2AG-B8A3.

As with many things, it all depends on the purpose the media is serving. But providing access to an alternate content form increases the accessibility of your content. The most important thing is that the content exists, is accounted for, and is made available to your users. It isn't trapped in some proprietary format that requires a user to have a specific technology or capability in order to access it.

Some folks might look at the Vanguard example and think the text is redundant in light of the graphic, but the reality is that it supports the graphic in numerous ways. We all learn and process stimuli differently—some of us are visual learners, some are verbal, and so on—and presenting the key information in multiple ways addresses this by providing alternate means of getting your messages across. Moreover, it ensures that no part of your message is lost.

Exploring Alternatives

The content embedded in any media type can and should be made available in an open, universally accessible format. For video and audio files, a transcript is often appropriate.[16] Videos can also be captioned.[17] For charts and graphs, it's typically data tables. For timelines and such, it's probably lists.

Images should be called out and have alternative text if they are important enough to warrant being called content. If they are purely decorative, leave their `alt` attributes blank or consider adding them via CSS. Icons can be meaningful. If they are, they need alternative text.

The PDF Conundrum

One major challenge on the Web is PDF (Portable Document Format). PDFs are often deployed on the Web when someone on the project thinks the content needs to be delivered in that one special format. But that's generally a weak argument. Few documents, apart from some legally restricted ones perhaps, require their content and layout be intrinsically tied the way they are in a PDF.

Have you ever tried reading a PDF on a mobile phone? Sure, it can be done, but it's not fun. Lots of pinching and zooming. It's also not fun to use 2.5MB of data to download a restaurant menu in PDF format that could easily have been good old fashioned HTML. And don't even get me started on PDF accessibility.[18]

---

16 There are a ton of reasonably priced services that do this. YouTube will even do it for you automatically, though the quality varies.

17 Accessibility expert Joe Clark has put together an amazing list of online captioning best practices: `http://perma.cc/X4UT-Y6V8`.

18 Accessibility expert Shawn Henry maintains a wealth of information about PDF accessibility and the accessibility of text in general at the TAdER project: `http://perma.cc/2G39-9MV5`.

Tying up your content in formats such as PDF is like tethering it to a giant anchor: It can't go anywhere easily or quickly. And anything you want to do with it requires a great deal of effort. When your content is rendered in HTML, however, it can travel hither and thither with the greatest of ease. It weighs little, it works on any device that can access the Web, and the content reflows to meet the user's needs. For free.

Spending a few moments thinking about making your content as broadly accessible as you can will pay huge dividends in the long run. It increases the accessibility of your content, improves the usability of your interfaces, and ensures the products you create will be able to reach your customers on any device, over any connection, anywhere in the world.

KEEP DATA ENTRY CONVERSATIONAL

When it comes to copy, few things are as boring, dry, or robotic as forms.

We often feel compelled to create forms that are very clinical. Perhaps it's because in the world of surveys we know too much "personality" can influence responses. But there's a difference between being personable and having an aggressive personality. In fact, I'd say there's a pretty wide chasm there.

You need to remember that you're authoring interfaces that will be used by real, honest-to-goodness people. When you're creating forms that don't require scientific rigor, you can (and should) do whatever you can to make the interaction more human. More *conversational*.

You should ask real questions: "What's your name?" and "What's your email?" and "How would you prefer we contact you?" are far more friendly than Name, Email, and Contact Preference. They're also completely unambiguous. Sure, it's unlikely, but it's entirely possible that someone could read Contact Preference and be unclear on what you want to know.

Clarity is important, and the words you choose matter. The Facebook story I shared earlier in this chapter is a perfect example of this. You need to think about how your interfaces *read*. You need to be deliberate in your word choices to avoid confusing your users. You need to know your audience and speak to them as they speak to you. That is the foundation of a great user experience.

DON'T FILL SPACE

They say nature abhors a vacuum, but nature has nothing on a website design committee.

Ever since the beginning of the Web, we have looked for ways to fill space. It was tougher when we were on 640×480 screens, but when we moved to 800×600, by golly we filled it up. 1024×768? Oh, we packed it in. 1920×1080? To the brim! Give us a vacant inch of screen real estate, and we'll find something to go there.

We know we shouldn't do it. Studies have shown that empty space helps refocus attention where you want it.[19] And yet, we cram more and more onto the page, all of which competes for attention. The more competition, the more exhausting the experience is for your users. When the distractions obscure the content, most users will just give up.

Thankfully, it doesn't have to be this way. By focusing on the purpose of your pages at every decision point, you can keep things from getting out of hand.

Some additional page bits are immutable: branding, navigation, copyright information, advertising. But then there's the other stuff

---

19 http://perma.cc/4S7H-62EC

we chuck into the page because we feel compelled to: social media buttons, possibly related articles, internal promotions, more advertising, newsletter sign-up forms, and even more advertising.

You need to take a hard look at what you put on the page and ask yourself that age-old question: Does this content actually add to the experience?

In some cases, it legitimately might. For instance, when someone finishes reading an article, it makes sense to offer them some related content options they might enjoy. Or maybe that's a place it makes sense to offer them a quick way to share the content on their social media network of choice. There's some consideration of the experience in those decisions.

By contrast, it makes no sense to put those sharing options right below the title of the article. The user hasn't even had a chance to read it; they don't even know if it's worth sharing yet!

By evaluating each page component through the lens of how it contributes to the page's purpose, you can keep your pages lean and give your users a more focused experience. Typically, this is an easy sell on mobile, where screen real estate is at a premium, but users on larger screens will benefit as well.

For a great example of how a company can shift from cluttered to clear, consider *Forbes*. In 2007, an article page on Forbes.com was more distraction than content (**Figure 2.7**). In 2015, its layout is far more focused (**Figure 2.8**). It's absolutely clear that the purpose of the page is getting their users to the content and making it a pleasure to read.

A design revolution like this doesn't happen by accident. A lot of thoughtful consideration went into designing an interface that is "less"—less cluttered, less disorienting, and less aggravating. The team was clearly focused and let content drive the experience.

Figure 2.7 *An article in Forbes circa 2007 (as captured for posterity by Merlin Mann). Everything that is not the content is grayed out.*

Figure 2.8 *An article in Forbes circa 2015 is far more focused on providing the article content.*

LET CONTENT LEAD THE WAY

Every website has a purpose, and every decision you make with respect to it should support that purpose. What do your users need to be able to do? How can you help them do that as easily and painlessly as possible? How can you ensure their experience is a good one? Experience starts with your content. All the technology in the world won't make your web project successful if the content lacks focus, clarity, and purpose.

Your interfaces are a conversation with your users, so you should always begin by thinking about how you want it to go. You need to think about how your contributions to the conversation can get your users the information they need in a way they can easily understand. And then you need to get out of the way.

Clear, well-written, and audience-appropriate content is the necessary baseline for progressive enhancement. Taking time to think it through early on will help you make better decisions down the road.

"HTML is the unifying language of the World Wide Web. Using just the simple tags it contains, the human race has created an astoundingly diverse network of hyperlinked documents, from Amazon, eBay, and Wikipedia, to personal blogs and websites dedicated to cats that look like Hitler. "

—JEREMY KEITH

CHAPTER 3:
MARKUP IS AN ENHANCEMENT

In 2005, when I was just starting to come to grips with web standards, I was tasked with leading the development end of a regional bank's website redesign. I was in charge of all the implementation details, from the content management system on the back end to the HTML templates, CSS, and JavaScript on the front end. It wasn't my first time overseeing a big project like that, but it was the first time I'd been given the opportunity to make every implementation decision…for better or for worse.

Web standards were by no means a new concept—the Web Standards Project had been advocating for them since 1998—but standards were only beginning to gain traction in the corporate world in the early 2000s. Wired News underwent a web standards–based redesign in 2002,[1] and ESPN.com shifted in 2003.[2] The

---

1   Designer Doug Bowman blogged about the project at
    http://perma.cc/G5KQ-4HDN.

2   Eric Meyer interviewed designer Mike Davidson about the project at
    http://perma.cc/6QEA-TYS2.

idea of jettisoning table-based layouts and spacer GIFs in favor of meaningful markup and CSS was only beginning to catch on.

I had been sold on the concept relatively early on, but I—like most of our industry—had been caught in the quicksand of corporate spaghetti code and Dreamweaver-driven templates, unable to drag myself out of the mire, at least not until this project came along.

I jumped headlong into the project and did everything I was supposed to do: semantic markup, CSS for layouts, optimized images, content-first source ordering, JavaScript for enhancement, and so on. No one else on the project seemed to care as much as I did about the "purity" of the code, but a few of my fellow developers thought it was cool how much CSS could do, even back then.

In the end, we delivered the project—on time and within budget, mind you—and our agency moved on to the next project. Sure, I felt the self-satisfaction of a job well done, but I doubt anyone else even noticed.

Then, about six months later, we were told that the bank had gone from page 10 in a Google search for "Connecticut bank" to the first page. In fact, it was the second result. The client—and our marketing team—was eager to know what wizardry we'd worked in the `meta` tags.

The answer: nothing.

In fact, I had forgotten to include the keyword and description `meta` tags entirely. And yet here we were with an astounding jump in the organic search rankings.

What was the secret sauce? Progressive enhancement.

Before the redesign, the site was a bit of a markup nightmare: Content was buried in deeply nested tables, much of the actual text of the site was trapped within images that lacked appropriate `alt` text, any actual text content was `font`-wrapped and bereft of meaning, and JavaScript was required for the primary navigation on the home page.

We turned this on its head and produced a series of clean and lean templates that used semantic elements such as heading levels and lists, paid attention to source order and the document outline, moved all the design into CSS, and used JavaScript to enhance the experience. Yeah, I forgot the `meta` tags, but it didn't matter because search engines love meaningful markup.[3]

In this chapter, you'll learn how to use markup to enhance your web pages. You'll see the importance of semantically appropriate elements, source order, the document outline, and accessibility. You'll also explore how you can use markup to supercharge your pages, delivering your content beyond the browser.

LEARN FROM THE PAST

When we first began building web pages, many of us didn't understand the purpose of markup. Those of us who came to the Web from a programming background often considered learning HTML beneath us, so we never put in the time to come to grips with the semantics it provided.

Those of us who came to the Web from a design background didn't understand the importance of semantics either. We thought only of the presentational aspect of a web page and latched on to the `table` element as a means of laying out pages in columns (CSS didn't exist at the time). Once we saw how `table` elements could be used to control layout, we found other ways to use them, often supplanting existing (and well-supported) semantic elements, such as lists and paragraphs (**Figure 3.1**).

---

3   http://perma.cc/D393-LF57

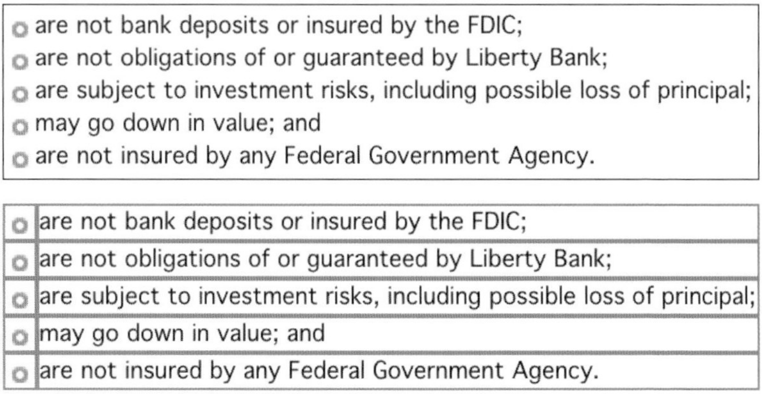

Figure 3.1 *We used* table *elements for everything back in the day. On top is a list, as displayed in the browser. Below shows the underlying table with the table cells outlined so you can see the structure. We should have just used an unordered list (* ul *).*

In offices across the globe, advocacy for using meaningful markup and CSS for presentation fell on deaf ears. The argument was seen as a largely idealistic one because, first, the fact remained that table–based layouts still worked in modern browsers and, second, the case for greater web accessibility was lost on many people who had no firsthand experience of using the Web with a disability. Then Google came along and changed everything. Suddenly, semantic markup was important.

Google was the first search engine to take semantics into account when indexing web pages. Starting with the humble anchor (a) element, which was the cornerstone of its original PageRank algorithm,[4] Google pioneered the use of semantic markup to infer meaning and relevancy.

The other search engines soon followed. As search engine spiders began hunting for other meaningful HTML elements on web pages (for example, the h1 element, which indicates the most important content on a page), semantic markup became more important to the business world. Proper semantics meant better search rankings and, thereby, a greater opportunity to attract new customers.

---

4   So-named for Google cofounder Larry Page, not because it ranked pages.

ILLUMINATE YOUR CONTENT

If content were soil, semantic markup would be the compost you'd add to ensure a productive garden. It enriches the content, providing your users with clues about intent and context, as well as supplementary information about the content itself.

Take, for example, the humble abbreviation element (`abbr`). It's used to denote abbreviations and acronyms.

```
Chattanooga, <abbr title="Tennessee">TN</abbr>
```

In this simple HTML snippet from my website, you can see how the abbreviation enhances the letters *TN* by informing the user that they stand for "Tennessee."

As HTML has evolved, its vocabulary has steadily expanded to offer more options for describing the content it encapsulates. The advent of HTML5 ushered in a slew of new semantic options (such as the `main` element, which is to denote the primary content of a page) and even augmented a few existing ones (such as the aforementioned `abbr` that took over for the ousted `acronym`).

As I mentioned in Chapter 2, the purpose of design is not to make something pretty; it's to clarify content or an idea. HTML excels at that. It takes the clear well-written prose that is the foundation of every online experience, and it illuminates the role each element plays in the interface. In short, the HTML you write matters.

MEAN WHAT YOU SAY

Every choice you make in building a website affects your users' experience. If you've worked on the Web for any amount of time, however, you're also well aware that there are always multiple ways to accomplish the same goal. For example, to create a button that can submit a form, you could use an `input`, a `button`, an `a`, or a `div` (or just about any other element). But not all these "buttons" are created equal.

ELEMENT	APPEARANCE	FOCUSABLE	TAPPABLE	SUBMITS FORMS
`input`	Button	Yes	Yes	If `type="submit"`
`button`	Button	Yes	Yes	If `type="submit"`
`a`	Inline text	Yes	Yes	No
`div`	Block text	No	No	No

Table 3.1 *A comparison of various elements and their native capacity to act like buttons.*

Compare the button-ness of these different elements in terms of how they are handled by default in a browser (**Table 3.1**).

As you can see, these elements act very differently in their default states. The `input` element and the `button` are as you would expect: They look like a button, they are focusable via the keyboard like a button, they are tappable/clickable, and they have the capacity to submit a form.

Anchor elements (`a`) are intended to function as anchor points in a document or as links to other pages. They are not meant to be buttons. Anchors are both focusable and tappable, but they lack the default appearance of a button, meaning CSS is required to achieve that. Anchors also cannot submit a form, which means you need to employ JavaScript to do that. Anchors are also activated only via the keyboard using the Enter key; true buttons can be activated by the spacebar as well. Listening for and acting on the additional key press also requires JavaScript.

In other words, to make an anchor element look and act like a button, you have added two dependencies you didn't have with an `input` or `button`: CSS and JavaScript. If either is not available, the interface will not operate as intended. That extra CSS and JavaScript is also more code that needs to be downloaded and executed in the browser, which affects the performance of the interface. Oh, and you need to maintain all of that extra code over time. Fun!

That brings us to the `div`. Semantically, a `div` is a generic "division" of the page. It's a vanilla box with no inherent design or behavior other than its contents begin on a new line (like a paragraph but with no default margins). This makes the `div` appealing if you want to fully customize an element to look and behave a particular way; you don't have to override the default look or behavior of the element, which can potentially save a few bits in your CSS or JavaScript.

The downside is that it's a vanilla box, meaning you get nothing for free (apart from the fact that it starts on its own line). To make the `div` a button, you need to do the following:

1. Make it look like a button, requiring CSS
2. Make it clickable like a button, requiring JavaScript
3. Make it keyboard focusable like a button, requiring the `tabindex` attribute
4. Make it keyboard interactive like a button, requiring JavaScript
5. Make it capable of submitting a form, also requiring JavaScript

So, while you have complete control over the element's visual appearance and behavior, an extra attribute is required, and CSS and JavaScript support are required for the `div` button to operate as intended.

Now with all of this in place, the `div` or `a` may look like a button and behave like a button, but as far as any computer or vision-impaired user is concerned, it's still not a button. The `a` version is a link (possibly to nowhere if the `href` value is "#" as it so often is in scenarios like this), and the `div` version is just some text. To indicate either is acting as a button, you need to add a `role` of "button" to the element.

The `role` attribute comes to HTML from the WAI-ARIA or ARIA, for short (Web Accessibility Initiative's Accessible Rich Internet Applications) spec.[5] ARIA is a collection of HTML attributes

---

5 http://perma.cc/4M28-77RS

that declare what is happening in the interface. Assistive technology looks for these clues to provide appropriate feedback for vision-impaired users. These attributes can also be useful hooks for simplifying your JavaScript. I'll touch on ARIA a bit more later in this chapter and in Chapter 5.

With a `role` of "button" declared on the `a` or `div`, the browser will know that the element in question is playing the part of a button in the interface. It doesn't get you anything additional, however; it just exposes the element as a button to assistive technology such as a screen reader.[6]

Avoid Introducing Fragility

Even with the `role` attribute, solidly authored CSS, and expertly written JavaScript in place, there are no guarantees that your user will be able to submit the form with the anchor (`a`) or `div`. Why? **Table 3.2** is a list of the dependencies and a few of the things that can go wrong.

Hmm, that's a pretty big list…it's a wonder any page works!

Granted, many of these are edge cases, but details matter. If you're running an ecommerce shop, you want a user to be able to make a purchase, no matter what. You need to erect as few barriers as possible that could prohibit them from accomplishing that task. If you use an `input` or a `button`, anyone will be able to submit an order, regardless. You can always use CSS and JavaScript to make the experience better, but they should serve to *enhance* the experience, not *be* the experience. I'll talk more about CSS and JavaScript in the next two chapters.

---

6 http://perma.cc/WB47-M8DJ

TECHNOLOGY	POTENTIAL ISSUE
CSS	The browser doesn't support CSS.
CSS	CSS is disabled for performance.
CSS	The user has altered CSS (via a user style sheet) for accessibility or some other personal preference.
CSS	A networking issue caused the CSS to be unavailable.
CSS	The selector is too advanced for the browser.
CSS	Rules appear in a media query and the browser doesn't support them.
JavaScript	The browser doesn't support JavaScript.
JavaScript	JavaScript is disabled.
JavaScript	A networking issue caused the JavaScript to be unavailable.
JavaScript	A firewall blocked requests for JavaScript.
JavaScript	A browser plugin blocked the JavaScript download or execution.
JavaScript	A third-party JavaScript error caused JavaScript execution to stop.
JavaScript	A bug in the code caused the JavaScript to stop executing.
JavaScript	The browser failed a feature detection test and exited the script early.
ARIA	The browser does not support ARIA.
ARIA	The assistive technology does not support ARIA.

Table 3.2 *Technological dependencies and potential blocks to their availability.*

As you can see, there are a lot of hoops to jump through to make one element look and behave like another. The trade-offs are rarely worth it. All you're doing by going down that path is building a more fragile, heavy, and difficult-to-maintain interface. And we've been looking at only a single button. Multiply the complexity of this one element by the number of interface elements you have on any given page, and you're probably starting to see why this isn't a great road to go down.

Each element has a purpose.[7] When you need a paragraph, you use a `p`. When you have a list of items, they each go in an `li` (for "list item"). If the items need to be in a particular order, they go inside an `ol` (for "ordered list"). If not, they go in a `ul` (for "unordered list").

You can use CSS to make these elements look however you want, so there is no reason to use a `div` when what you really need is a `p`, for example. It was a lesson many of us had to learn back in the olden days when we were abusing tables to no end. I can't count the number of times I used a two-column `table` when I should have used a list.[8]

When you use an element for its intended purpose, you enhance the meaning of your content: You use `h1` to indicate the most important headline on the page and `h6` to indicate the least important headline on the page; you use `em` to add emphasis to a word; you use `strong` to indicate that phrase is important; and you use `code` to indicate, well, code. Markup enriches your content and reduces the ambiguity of plain text.

---

7   http://perma.cc/J2LH-J3WG

8   I would put the bullet in the first column of the table and the text in the second column (like you saw in Figure 3.1) to control the margins and padding and to get the bullets to line up nicely with the top of the text. I'd also use an image for the bullets. *Table with two columns and five rows—* which is what a screen reader says—obscures the fact that it's a list and obscures the number of items. *List of five items* is perfectly clear. I should have used an unordered list and some CSS. *Oh, the humanity!*

In one final example, consider the last sentence in footnote 8. I'd probably mark up "Oh, the humanity!" in an `i` element because if I were to read that paragraph aloud to you, I'd say that in a slightly sarcastic way. The `i` element is for content that is in an alternate voice or mood. One day in the future, I'll even be able to use CSS Speech (formerly "aural" style sheets) to prompt a synthesized voice—such as a screen reader or digital assistant—to speak that sentence differently.

When you put more thought into your markup—by making more deliberate element choices—you clarify the meaning of your words, make your content more expressive, and create more opportunities to improve your users' experiences.

EMBRACE CLASSIFICATION AND IDENTIFICATION

Choosing the right element is the crucial first step in progressively enhancing a web page. Once you've done that, you can take things a bit further with attributes.

Some elements, such as the `a` you saw earlier, require attributes in order to serve their purpose. An `a` without its `href` would not provide a link to anywhere. Other attributes are optional, like the `role` attribute you saw in the discussion of buttons.

Two attributes in particular are used to extend HTML's native semantics in a less formal way. I'm talking, of course, about `id` and `class`.

When the W3C's Dave Raggett drafted a specification for HTML 3.0,[9] it contained two new concepts: classification and identification, expressed via the `class` and `id` attributes, respectively.[10] These two attributes were not formally introduced into the HTML lexicon until HTML 4.0 but were implemented in browsers around the same time as CSS support was added. And CSS, of course, brought us two simple selectors that targeted these attributes explicitly, causing some unfortunate confusion over the intended use of `class` and `id` from the get-go.

For years, nearly every web designer—myself included—thought the correlation between the attributes and the selectors was intentional. We believed that `id` and `class` were intended purely for use with CSS. You can't blame us, though: At the time CSS didn't provide many ways to select elements. It made sense that `class` (e.g., `.menu`) and `id` (e.g., `#content`) would have been introduced so we could style elements both generally and specifically.[11]

Thankfully, we now understand how `class` and `id` were meant to operate. The `class` attribute was introduced specifically to address the limited set of elements within HTML.

> *As time goes by, people's expectations change, and more will be demanded of HTML. One manifestation of this is the pressure to add yet more tags. HTML 3.0 introduces a means for subclassing elements in an open-ended way. This can be used to distinguish the role of a paragraph element as being a couplet in a stansa*

---

9   HTML 3.0 (`http://perma.cc/RHG6-V5AJ`) was an ambitious draft: It introduced numerous tags and attributes. Many of the new elements were dropped by the time it reached recommendation status as HTML 3.2, but the `class` and `id` attributes survived. Interestingly enough, some of the same constructs proposed in HTML 3.0 have found their way back into HTML, either formally as part of HTML5 or quasiformally as microformats.

10   It's worth noting that `class` and `id` each make a (very) brief appearance in the HTML 2 spec (`http://perma.cc/Y583-YSQF`) but were not formally defined attributes. They were simply used to demonstrate the fault-tolerant way in which browsers should treat unknown attributes.

11   And the HTML 3 draft did allow for this use, among others.

[sic], or a mathematical term as being a tensor. This ability to make fresh distinctions can be exploited to impart distinct rendering styles or to support richer search mechanisms, without further complicating the HTML document format itself.[12]

The intent was that `class` would contain a list of subclasses for that particular element, with the classes listed from most general to most specific.[13] In this example, the generic division is being sub-classed as a "promotional module" (as it goes in order from least specific to most specific).[14]

```
<div class="module promotional">
  ...
</div>
```

The `id` attribute was created for the purpose of identifying a specific element on the page. Each `id` is expected to be unique on a given page. Identifiers can be used as a reference point for CSS selection (e.g., `#details`), scripts (e.g., `document.getElementById('details')`), and anchors (e.g., `<a href="#details">`).

The `class` and `id` attributes allow page authors to add their own semantics on top of those defined in the HTML spec. Together, these ad hoc semantics imbue the markup with greater meaning and, over time, have gravitated toward a common set of classifications and identifiers in use across the globe (e.g., `#header`, `#nav`, and `.article`). This common set of classifications and identifiers

---

12 From the "Scalability" section of the HTML 3 draft.

13 You'll see this throughout the HTML 3 draft, whenever `class` is defined for an element.

14 If you've heard at all about the Block-Element-Modifier (BEM) methodology developed by Yandex, its concept of a modifier tracks quite closely to this idea, but in BEM it is a bit more explicit (`http://perma.cc/L3WQ-9GW5`). The nature of subclassing in this example (exemplified by the *block--modifier* syntax) draws direct connections between the "module" subclass and its "promotional" variant. BEM is an interesting approach to classification that's grown on me the more I've used it.

has, in turn, provided valuable guidance in the continued evolution of HTML, resulting in many new elements (e.g., `header`, `nav`, and `article`). They also fostered the development of a community-driven set of HTML conventions known as *microformats*.

Use Microformats to Empower Tools

Microformats are a set of community-driven specifications for how to mark up content to expose semantics (and metadata) that are not available in HTML. Microformats formalize organically developed `class`-based naming conventions into a specification that addresses a need not met by HTML. For example, HTML provides no robust way to mark up contact information or events, so the community created microformats to make that possible.

The first microformat arose from a desire to express associations between individuals on the Web and was called XFN (XHTML Friends Network). Though not developed as a "microformat" (that term came later), XFN was a perfect example of extending the semantics of HTML with a specific goal in mind.

Developed by web standards advocate Tantek Çelik, WordPress creator Matt Mullenweg, and CSS wizard Eric Meyer, XFN makes use of the oft-neglected `rel` attribute. The purpose of `rel`—which you are probably familiar with in the context of `rel="stylesheet"` when including external CSS files—is to indicate the relationship of the target of an `href` attribute to the current page.

The idea was simple: If I wanted to point from my blog to the blog of a colleague, I could employ XFN and add `rel="colleague"` to the link. Similarly, if I was linking to my wife's blog, I would use `rel="friend co-resident spouse muse sweetheart co-worker"` because she is all of those things.[15]

---

15   And more. *Awwww.*

On its own, this additional markup does little more than provide a bit more information about our relationship and why I might be linking to another website, but if I use it for every link in my blog roll and those people, in turn, use it in theirs, all of a sudden we've created a network that is programmatically navigable, creating myriad opportunities for data mining and repurposing.

And that's exactly what happened: XFN spread like wildfire. Software developers integrated it into popular blogging tools (e.g., WordPress, Movable Type) and developers at nearly every site on the "social Web" (e.g., Twitter, Flickr, Last.fm) began adorning user profile pages with the special case of `rel="me"` (used to link from one web page you control to another), enabling tools like Google's Social Graph to quickly build a full profile of their users starting from a single URL.[16]

From that simple (yet powerful) beginning, microformats have increased in number to address common and diverse needs. Most use a specific set of `class` names to mark up content like a person's profile (h-card), event listings (h-event), content for syndication (h-feed), and resumes (h-resume). Others build off the `rel` attribute as XFN did: rel-license to indicate licensing information, rel-nofollow to control search engine spidering, and rel-tag to enable taxonomic tagging.[17]

Almost in parallel with the development of these microformats, numerous tools sprung up to make use of them. Search engines pay attention to them and, in many cases, even rank microformatted content higher than non-microformatted content.[18] Browser add-ons enable users to extract and repurpose microformatted content. Microformat parsers are also available for nearly every programming language out there, and there are even web-based services that give users direct access to the microformats in use

---

16 Sadly, Google killed its Social Graph product in 2012.

17 The Microformats.org wiki keeps a running list of all microformats and documentation on how to use them.

18 `http://perma.cc/ZA7G-NSKG`

on their sites. Read-it-later services such as Readability also use microformats to extract content reliably from web pages.

Here's a quick example of an h-card:

```
<span class="h-card">Aaron Gustafson</span>
```

Based on this markup—essentially, the inclusion of the h-card `class`—a microformats parser knows the page contains a reference to a person and that person's name is Aaron Gustafson. This is a slightly more complicated example:

```
<a class="h-card"
   href="http://www.aaron-gustafson.com">...</a>
```

I say slightly because it's not really all that more complicated. But now, the microformats parser knows the page includes a reference to a person, and it knows their name and URL.

Microformats are yet another layer in the progressive enhancement continuum, enabling you to make your sites even more useful to your users. After all, how cool is it that you can enable your users to export an event to their calendar or a business card to their address book directly from your web page? That's pretty slick. And, as an added bonus—if, like me, you vacillate over `class` names—microformats provide a set of predefined values to handle a variety of common scenarios.

Take It Further with RDFa and Microdata

If microformats get you excited about the possibilities of adding machine-readable hints and metadata to your documents but you don't find them rich or flexible enough, you'll probably love RDFa and microdata. These two technologies provide alternative ways to imbue HTML (and XML and SVG, etc.) with structured data. They are alternatives to microformats but can often play nicely with them too.

I used a microdata vocabulary to describe a book[19] on the web page for the first edition of this tome.[20] First, I set things up on the `html` element.

```
<html lang="en" itemscope
      itemtype="http://schema.org/Book">
```

Adding the `itemscope` attribute set the whole page as the scope of the object being described, and `itemtype` pointed to the Book vocabulary I was using from Schema.org. With that basic stuff in place, I just added one more tag and two more attributes to identify specific bits of content for extraction. The `itemprop` attribute is the key to identifying pieces of the object.

- I added a `meta` element with `itemprop="image"` and pointed to the URL for the book cover image in the `content` attribute.
- I added `itemprop="name"` to the `h1` element for the book's title, and I added `itemprop="description"` to a paragraph I felt best summarized the book.

It was surprisingly simple to implement given how difficult the documentation on Schema.org is to parse (at least to me).

RDFa is a bit more rigorous and formal than microformats and microdata. A good example of RDFa in practice is the Open Graph protocol created by Facebook.[21] Incidentally, you can also find Open Graph in use on that same page, serving the same general function. Here's a representative sampling:

---

19 I used the vocabulary from Schema.org, a collaboration between Google, Microsoft, Yahoo, and Yandex intended to improve search results.

20 `http://perma.cc/G26T-WKUS`

21 `http://perma.cc/7YXW-UFQ3`

```
<meta property="og:type" content="book">
<meta property="og:title"
      content="Adaptive Web Design">
<meta property="og:image" content="cover.png">
<meta property="og:description"
      content="In this brief...">
```

As with the microdata example, these `meta` tags enable a web crawler to easily extract key information from the document. Facebook, Google+, Twitter, LinkedIn, and others use the OpenGraph tags to create the preview you see when you link to a website in a post. Twitter has also created its own RDFa tags to build upon the Open Graph protocol in service of its Twitter Cards effort.[22] Similarly, Pinterest drives its Rich Pins feature with Open Graph tags.[23]

You can embed RDFa outside of `meta` tags too, using the `vocab`, `typeof`, and `property` attributes. RDFa Play[24] provides a nice isolated testing environment that helps you see how your RDFa objects come together. Google also offers an incredibly handy structured data testing tool,[25] which can expose your microdata, RDFa, and microformatted objects.

When adding structured data like this, you supercharge your HTML documents, making already well-structured, easily indexed content even more useful to search engines and other computer-based tools by identifying the most useful bits using a more formal naming structure. Structured data empowers your content to go far beyond the browser, and that's another perfect example of progressive enhancement.

---

22 http://perma.cc/K56A-QWCH

23 http://perma.cc/D27X-YF53

24 http://perma.cc/Z6LT-7HBJ

25 http://perma.cc/96LS-7N4X

MAKE DELIBERATE MARKUP CHOICES

There are times when you may legitimately need to insert semantically unnecessary markup into your documents. Most often, it's when you need to group somewhat-related elements to lay out the page properly with CSS. Traditionally, you'd use generic div elements for this purpose and give them semantic class names such as "section," "article," or "aside." With the advent of HTML5, we were given first-class elements that serve those purposes: section, article, aside, header, footer, and main. Using these elements, you can make wrappers like this purposeful, intentional.

You should try to avoid adding unnecessary markup as often as possible to keep your pages smaller and faster to load. To achieve this, I often start marking up the content of a page using only content-related elements such as p and ul. Then, I look for natural ways to group those elements into related chunks (**Figure 3.2**). In forms, you have the handy fieldset for aggregating related form controls, but outside of forms you can use article or section for that purpose.

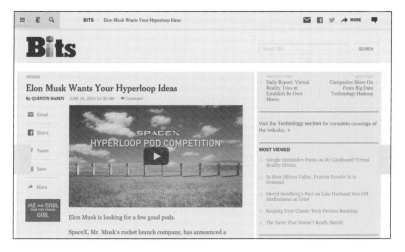

Figure 3.2 *A New York Times article page with organizationally linked content grouped into colored blocks.*

These two elements are pretty similar but serve different purposes. A `section` is just what you'd think: a portion of some larger piece of content (for instance, the chapter you're reading is a *section* of this book). An `article` is best thought of as an autonomous unit of content—it can exist on its own. A good rule of thumb for using these elements is that if the content in question could be removed from the document without affecting the meaning of either the document or the content itself, `article` is your best bet. If it can't, it's a `section`.

Interestingly (and somewhat confusingly), a `section` can contain one or more `article` or `section` descendants, and an `article` can contain one or more `section` or `article` descendants. But if you keep coming back to the `article` being an independent unit of content, you'll always make the right call.

Honor the Outline

While visually `article` and `section` are no different than a `div`, from a semantic standpoint they do have an effect on the page. The `article` and `section` elements, along with `nav` and `aside`, are referred to as *sectioning* elements because they divide the document in an explicit way. The concept of explicit sectioning came about in HTML5 as a way of overcoming the limitation of having only six heading elements (`h1`–`h6`).

The `h1`–`h6` elements generate a natural document outline,[26] which enables a browser to create a table of contents for assistive technology to use in order to ease navigation around the page (**Figure 3.3**). The document outline can also be accessed programmatically by search engines to help them generate better search results. I've even accessed the document outline with JavaScript to enable me to turn static content into a dynamic tabbed interface.[27]

---

26 The Web Developer Toolbar (`http://perma.cc/B88J-6AET`) is an excellent browser add-on and features easy access to the document outline.

27 `http://perma.cc/J4KQ-T88R`

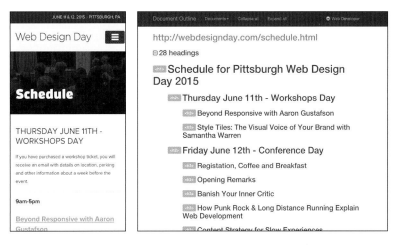

Figure 3.3 *The Web Design Day 2015 Schedule* (`http://perma.cc/E68X-R36B`) *and its corresponding document outline.*

The document outline provides an easy way to review the organization of your web pages and validate your source order decisions. It helps you ensure the content flow works.

As I mentioned, HTML defines only six heading levels. In some cases, that may not be enough to accommodate your document; once you need to go to a seventh level, you're out of options. Another problem this causes is that in a world of CMSs and componentized templates, maintaining control over the document outline can be painful. For instance, if article teasers came below an h1 on the home page but they came below an h2 in the sidebar of an article (**Figure 3.4**), you would need to have the teaser title marked up in an h2 in the first instance and an h3 in the second to maintain a proper outline.

To address these two use cases, explicit "sectioning elements" were added to HTML. In theory, these elements create a nested level in the document outline and allow you to start with h1 all over again. The reason I say "in theory" is that no browser has implemented the accessibility aspect of this approach yet. That doesn't mean they won't in the future; I'm hopeful because explicit sectioning is a useful feature in HTML.

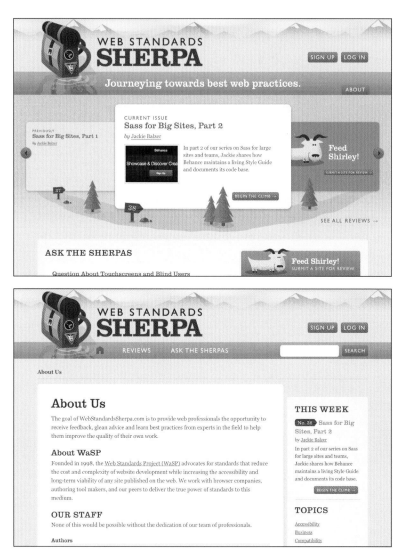

Figure 3.4 *The same article teaser used in two different places on Web Standards Sherpa. In the top image, the teaser is featured front and center. In the bottom image, it's a promotion in the sidebar.*

Look at the difference. Without sectioning elements, you would create a good document outline like this:

```
<h1>Ask the Sherpas</h1>
<h2>Question About Touchscreens and Blind Users</h2>
<!-- teaser content -->
<h2>Question About Rounded Corners and Progressive
    Enhancement</h2>
<!-- teaser content -->
```

But with sectioning elements, you have a bit more flexibility because you are being explicit about the outline.

```
<h1>Ask the Sherpas</h1>
<article>
 <h1>Question About Touchscreens and Blind
     Users</h1>
 <!-- teaser content -->
</article>
<article>
 <h1>Question About Rounded Corners and Progressive
     Enhancement</h1>
 <!-- teaser content -->
</article>
```

And in both instances the document outline would be as follows:

1. Ask the Sherpas
   a. Question About Touchscreens and Blind Users
   b. Question About Rounded Corners and Progressive Enhancement

If your website isn't terribly complex so as to require more than six heading levels and you have the flexibility in your CMS, I'd advise you to use the traditional outlining algorithm as your guide while still using sectioning elements. This allows the outline to remain the same under either outlining algorithm.

```
<h1>Ask the Sherpas</h1>
<article>
 <h2>Question About Touchscreens and Blind Users</h2>
 <!-- teaser content -->
</article>
<article>
 <h2>Question About Rounded Corners and Progressive
     Enhancement</h2>
 <!-- teaser content -->
</article>
```

The reason it works is that explicit sections treat the first heading level they encounter as the top heading level for that section. In other words, if you kick off an `article` with `h2` (as I just showed you), the `h2` would be equivalent to an `h1` in the same position (or an `h3`, `h4`, and so on). This approach ensures that the most users are served, both now and in the future.

One final note regarding sectioning elements and the outline: If you use a sectioning element, make sure it contains a heading. In other words, **never do this**:

```
<section>
 <article>
   <h2>Question About Touchscreens and Blind
       Users</h2>
   <!-- teaser content -->
 </article>
 <article>
   <h2>Question About Rounded Corners and
       Progressive Enhancement</h2>
   <!-- teaser content -->
 </article>
</section>
```

The outer `section` must have a heading inside it before the `article` elements or else you end up with a broken outline:

1. MISSING HEADLINE
    a. Question About Touchscreens and Blind Users
    b. Question About Rounded Corners and Progressive Enhancement

You can always use CSS to hide the headline if you don't want to show it. Or if no headline is really needed, maybe it isn't worthy of being a distinct `section` element after all; maybe it's merely a division (`div`). Or maybe—in place of a container and a heading—a paragraph-level thematic break (`hr`) makes the most sense. Each situation is different. Weigh the options and their implications and then make the decision.

Be Intentional with Source Order

As discussed in Chapter 2, the interfaces you create are a conversation with your users. When you consider it in that light, it becomes easy to make smarter decisions in terms of the source order you use for your pages.

A classic design tension is where to place the navigation for your site in terms of source order. Some argue that navigation should come right after the site branding because users may want immediate access to the navigational links to find what they are looking for. Others argue that the content of the page is the priority and should therefore come before the navigation.

On most pages, I find the latter approach to be more beneficial, and here's why: If I am having a conversation with someone, that conversation is my priority. Navigation ends the conversation by forcing someone to make a choice, possibly before they are even informed enough to feel like they can make a good one.

In his book *Mobile First*, Luke Wroblewski furthers this argument with a focus on mobile devices (where screen real estate is at a premium).

As a general rule, content takes precedence over navigation on mobile. Whether people are checking on frequently updated data like stocks, news, or scores; looking up local information; or finding their way to articles through search or communication tools—they want immediate answers to their needs and not your site map.

Too many mobile web experiences…start the conversation off with a list of navigation options instead of content. Time is often precious on mobile and downloads can cost money, so get people to what they came for as soon as you can.[28]

When you consider the continuum of experience moving from the smallest screens to the largest ones, the decisions you make need to support those smaller screen experiences first. Users come to your site for the content, not your navigation.

This approach may also have some benefits when it comes to SEO (search engine optimization). Much of the world of SEO is voodoo and black magic—search engines don't often want the inner workings of their web crawlers or indexing algorithms to be made public because people would quickly use that information to game their rankings. That said, the web crawlers that search engines employ do tend to reward thoughtful choices for source order as they do other deliberate markup choices. For example, the following gives greater weight to content that appears farther up in the page:[29]

[T]he placement of your keywords matters far more than their frequency. Posting "auto repair shop" once in the title tag of your site and once in the header matters far more than stuffing it five times into the body copy. Google breaks your site down into key areas, with meta information and headers taking top priority, body copy taking secondary priority, and side bars and footers taking the last priority.

---

28 http://perma.cc/YK62-DWGV

29 http://perma.cc/S3TB-C6NS

In my experience, making decisions that are in your users' best interests often yield SEO benefits organically, so I don't spend much time focusing on SEO-related recommendations. But if you need the extra ammunition for discussing source order with a team member, this is a good argument to have at the ready.

Although it happens less frequently now—with users' increased reliance on search engines—it's worth noting that there are instances where a user may land on the home page for a site and need to browse or search for content. In this instance, it's quite handy to have quick access to the navigation. But if the navigation is at the bottom of a long page on a mobile screen, all that scrolling could be frustrating.

Thankfully, all is not lost. Remember that `id` attributes can function as anchor reference points in the document. That means if you give your navigation an `id` of "nav," you can simply include an anchor to the navigation right after the branding. You can see this approach in use on the *Contents Magazine* website (**Figure 3.5**).

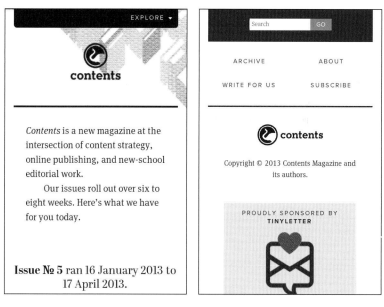

Figure 3.5 Contents Magazine's *website* (http://perma.cc/MC93-N5D2) *with a link anchoring to the navigation. A video version is available at* http://perma.cc/P4S9-RVW2.

Here's a simplified version of what is going on in this site:

```html
<header>
 <!-- logo -->
 <p><a href="#site-nav">Explore</a></p>
</header>

<!-- page content -->

<div id="site-nav">
 <!-- search form -->
 <nav>
   <ul>
     <li><a href="/articles/">Archive</a></li>
     <!-- nav continues -->
   </ul>
 </nav>
</div>

<!-- site footer -->
```

You can take this a step further by facilitating movement back up the page as well. After the navigation, offer a link to the content of the page. Nichols College[30] does that. You'll examine this approach and how they used CSS to enhance that experience to great effect in Chapter 4.

On larger screens, most websites place the navigation of a page above the content, which may also seem problematic. But with CSS, there are myriad ways to rearrange the page and move the navigation above the content.

Source order matters. It has a direct effect on the usability of your pages, and navigation versus content is only one example of how this can play out. There are countless other small-scale instances where you need to pay attention to source order. Consider a blog post: It

---

30 http://perma.cc/3H32-9GBH

wouldn't make sense to offer a list of links to related posts until after the user has read the post they're on. Similarly, it doesn't make sense to ask them to share it on social media until they've actually read it.

The document outline (discussed earlier) is a great tool for getting an at-a-glance view of your overall page's organization, but there really is no substitute for reading your source. Search engines and assistive technologies experience your content in this way, so you should too. If the order of your elements makes sense as you are reading the interface, then you are well on your way to providing a usable and accessible experience.

Avoid Unnecessary Markup

Another situation in which you might feel the need to add extra markup is when you are coding interactive widgets. Consider a tabbed interface, for example (**Figure 3.6**). To build a tabbed interface, you need some specific elements in your markup. Here's a simplified version of the markup from that page:

```
<div class="tabbed-interface">
  <ol class="tablist">
    <li class="tab">Target Type</li>
    <li class="tab">Therapy Type</li>
  </ol>
  <section class="tabpanel">
    <h1 class="hidden">Target Type</h1>
    <table>
      <!-- table contents -->
    </table>
  </section>
  <section class="tabpanel">
    <h1 class="hidden">Therapy Type</h1>
    <table>
      <!-- table contents -->
    </table>
  </section>
</div>
```

| TARGET TYPE | THERAPY TYPE | | | | | | | | | | | |
Target Types	Timeline	Phase 1/2	Phase 1	Phase 2	Phase 2/3	Phase 3	Phase 4	Approved	Inactive	Discontinued	Not Regulated	Total
Amyloid-Related		1	6	15	4	4	0	0	3	12	0	45
Cholesterol		0	1	0	0	0	1	0	1	0	0	3
Cholinergic System		0	1	2	0	1	0	4	5	11	0	24
Inflammation		0	1	5	3	2	0	0	1	8	0	20
Other		0	3	23	2	4	3	0	4	8	0	47
Other Neurotransmitters		0	1	7	0	2	1	1	1	11	0	24
Tau		0	4	0	0	1	0	0	1	3	0	9
Unknown		0	0	6	0	1	1	0	3	3	0	14

Figure 3.6 *A tabbed interface on AlzForum.org*
(`http://perma.cc/BR3X-R7ZS`).

To make the tabbed interface functional, it needs tabs to click on
(`li.tab`), a tab list to contain them (`ol.tablist`), and content panels to show and hide (`section.tabpanel`). But a tabbed interface requires JavaScript to function, so if the JavaScript enhancement is not available, a user has to contend with this crufty markup, which may be confusing. It's also additional markup that has to be downloaded, and it has to be maintained by people like us. What happens if six months down the road you decide to ditch tabbed interfaces on your site in favor of accordions? You'd need to rip all this code out of your documents. Lame!

When you encounter situations like this—where you need extra markup to enable JavaScript-based functionality—it pays to recognize the potential usability and maintainability issues with hard-coding the extra markup. Rather than hard-coding it, you can use JavaScript to generate that markup only when you need it.

JavaScript is really good at manipulating HTML documents, so it is no problem for it to yank out pieces of markup and dynamically assemble the HTML you need to create a tabbed interface. That is exactly what happens on AlzForum.org: The page authors used a `class` of "tabbed-interface" to inform JavaScript that the content within should be transformed into a tabbed interface, but that's the only bit that's hard-coded; the tabbed interface is entirely built using JavaScript. The script then reads out the headings it encounters within—which, per my earlier recommendation, would be better as `h3` rather than `h1` elements—and dynamically constructs the tabbed interface from there.

From a user's standpoint, the experience is positive whether JavaScript is available because the linearized content is perfectly usable. From a maintenance standpoint, it becomes inconsequential to make updates to the tabbed interface markup because it's generated by a single script. Finally, if they ever wanted to get rid of the tabbed interfaces, they could either remove the "tabbed-interface" `class` names or simply remove that particular JavaScript from the site.

I'll dissect the tabbed interface on AlzForum and talk more about using JavaScript to progressively enhance pages in Chapter 5.

CLARIFY INTERFACES WITH ARIA

Early in this chapter, I introduced the ARIA `role` attribute as a way to make one element behave as another as far as assistive technology is concerned. Remember the `div` masquerading as a `button`? There is a specific subset of `role` values that act as landmarks within a document that assistive technology can expose and allow a user to jump from one part of the page to another. **Table 3.3** lists a few examples.

Some of these roles directly correlate with existing HTML elements (e.g., `main`, `aside`, and `nav`), which can seem a little confusing. The reason for this is twofold. First, the ARIA spec and HTML5, which introduced these corresponding elements, were developed independently at roughly the same time, so they address some of the very same issues. Second, there are instances where you may want one element to act as another (as in the `div` button example or in non-HTML markup like SVG where the same semantics don't exist). In other words, there are times the redundancy can be quite useful.

ROLE	INDICATES
`banner`	The header for the page (containing the site name, etc.)
`main`	The primary content of the page
`contentinfo`	The footer information for the page (containing site copyright, etc.)
`complementary`	Content related to but not part of the primary page content
`navigation`	Where to find navigational links
`search`	Where to find the search form for the site

Table 3.3 *A Few ARIA* `role` *Values and Their Meaning*

Whenever possible, you should follow the First Rule of ARIA Use.[31]

> *If you* can *use a native HTML element or attribute with the semantics and behaviour you require **already built in**, instead of re-purposing an element and adding an ARIA role, state or property to make it accessible, **then do so**.*

In other words, use the `main` element rather than `role="main"`, use `button` rather than `role="button"`, and so on. Now, interestingly, the ARIA landmarks that don't have direct semantic equivalents become a gateway for new elements to be exposed to assistive technology via the accessibility API. The landmark of `main` is a perfect example of this: The ARIA role predated the `main` element, and because it did, the ARIA mapping already existed to expose its semantic meaning. So when the `main` element came along, its mappings just piggybacked on the ARIA mapping, and it was supported by assistive technology on day one.[32]

---

31 This rule and other helpful guidelines are available in the W3C's Notes on Using ARIA in HTML (`http://perma.cc/JHL6-MBJZ`).

32 For more, see `http://perma.cc/DG6Z-LSDE`.

ARIA offers a rich set of roles, beyond the landmark ones, that allow you to clarify the function an element is playing in an interface.[33] Some map directly to existing HTML elements (e.g., "button", "listitem"), others are wholly unique to ARIA (e.g., "tablist", "tree"), but all are intended to help users better understand what is going on in the interface they are using.

I'll cover some of the widget-related roles (as well as ARIA's states and properties) in Chapter 5, but there are two unique ARIA roles I want to touch on before we move on.

The "alert" `role` indicates content that the user should be made aware of immediately. A good use case for using this `role` is to highlight form errors that are being returned from the server. This is the sort of content you want your users (especially your non-sighted ones) to be made aware of immediately. A closely related `role` is "alert dialog," which is like "alert" but the initial focus is taken to an element inside of it.

The "presentation" `role` removes any semantic meaning an element would otherwise have. In other words, it tells assistive technology to treat it as purely presentational (as opposed to meaningful). This isn't a `role` you're likely to need often, but it's useful in rare cases, for instance when hiding a presentational image from assistive technology. It's worth noting that this `role` is ignored if you apply it to an interactive element like a `button` or an anchor.

While ARIA roles are not required in your markup, they go a long way toward clarifying the purpose key elements serve within your interfaces, further enhancing the experience for users who can benefit from them.

---

33 A complete list is available at `http://perma.cc/39LA-6P7U`.

UNDERSTAND FAULT TOLERANCE

Progressive enhancement in HTML is possible because of one key feature of the language: fault tolerance. As I mentioned in Chapter 1, fault tolerance makes it possible to browse an HTML5-based website in Lynx. But how is that possible? Lynx originally came out in 1992, and HTML5 wasn't finalized until 2014.

It's simple: Browsers are instructed to ignore what they don't understand. When it comes to HTML, that means elements that aren't understood are ignored, but their contents are exposed. Unrecognized attributes are simply ignored.[34]

When I started building websites, it wasn't something that came up often. Then Flash came along[35] and, early on, the default way to include a Flash movie in your HTML was to do something akin to the following:

```
<object ...>
  <param name="movie" value="movie.swf">
  <!-- more param elements -->
  <embed src="movie.swf" ...>
</object>
```

This weird construct of an `embed` element nested within an `object` element had me perplexed. According to the HTML spec, `embed` wasn't even a valid element,[36] so what was it doing inside the `object`?

As it turned out, `embed` was a proprietary tag created by Netscape to allow plugin content to be run in a web page.[37] The W3C had

---

34 http://perma.cc/DU94-4JJC

35 Remember Flash?!

36 It is now.

37 Interestingly, Netscape founder Marc Andreessen is also credited with the creation of the once-proprietary `img` element, which he included in Mosaic (he also worked on that early browser), much to the chagrin of Tim Berners-Lee and others on the HTML mailing list in 1993.

standardized on the `object` element for embedding generic multimedia content of any kind. To serve both Netscape and Internet Explorer (the two dominant browsers at the time), Macromedia decided to use both.

This is where the fault-tolerant nature of HTML came into play: By wrapping the `object` element around the `embed`, the `object` would be encountered first. Browsers that understood the `object` element would insert the Flash movie and throw away the `embed` (since `object` allows only for `param` and other `object` elements inside it). Browsers that didn't understand `object` would ignore that element and move into its content, encountering the `embed`. If they understood the `embed` element, they would display the Flash movie. Browsers that didn't understand `embed` either would show nothing.

HTML is pretty brilliant in this way because it allows you to continue advancing the language without crippling older browsers' ability to display web pages. Let's look at a few more examples of fault tolerance in action, starting with another multimedia object: `video`.

The `video` element is a lot like `object` in that it allows you to embed video files natively (rather than relying on a Flash wrapper as we did for many years). The `video` element comes in two flavors: a single tag version for when the video is available only in a single format and a version with opening and closing tags that lets you supply multiple video format options.

```
<video src="movie.mp4" controls
       poster="movie.jpg">

<video controls poster="movie.jpg">
 <source src="movie.ogg" type="video/ogg">
 <source src="movie.mp4" type="video/mp4">
</video>
```

Since you know browsers that don't support the `video` element will ignore it, the latter offers you a bit more flexibility to provide fallbacks.

```
<video controls poster="movie.jpg">
 <source src="movie.ogg" type="video/ogg">
 <source src="movie.mp4" type="video/mp4">
 <p>I'm sorry, we can't play this video in
    your browser. Do you want to download
    it instead?</p>
 <ul>
   <li><a download href="movie.ogg">Ogg Theora
       Format</a></li>
   <li><a download href="movie.mp4">MP4
       Format</a></li>
 </ul>
</video>
```

Now, if a browser comes along and doesn't grok `video`, you have provided a nice message and offered them download links instead. But if `video` is supported in their browser, they just see the video. You can (and should) use this same approach for the `audio` element too. You may have noticed that I also included the `download` attribute on the links in the fallback. This causes supporting browsers to automatically download the linked content rather than navigate to it when a user clicks the anchor. That saves users from having to right-click the link to download the file.

The `picture` element was modeled on `video` and gives you the ability to define multiple art-directed images to be displayed in different media query-defined contexts. Its markup should look pretty familiar.

```
<picture>
 <source media="(min-width: 38em)"
         srcset="large.jpg">
 <source media="(min-width: 23em)"
         srcset="medium.jpg">
 <img src="small.jpg"
      alt="Aaron giving you a thumbs-up!">
</picture>
```

As you can probably guess, browsers that don't support `picture` will display the nested `img` element, but browsers that understand `picture` would use the source information to create an adaptive image.

There's another adaptive image option too: `srcset` and `sizes` applied to an `img`. Here's an example:

```
<img src="small.jpg" sizes="100vw"
     srcset="small.jpg 400w, medium.jpg 800w,
             large.jpg 1600w"
     alt="Aaron giving you a double thumbs-up!">
```

Browsers that support both the `srcset` and `sizes` attributes will download the most appropriate image given the width of the browser window.[38] Browsers that don't will ignore those attributes and use `img` in the traditional way by loading the image indicated in the `src` attribute.

Switching gears a little, consider form elements. Have you ever misspelled the value of a `type` attribute on an `input` before? You know, "chekbox" instead of "checkbox" or "adio" instead of "radio"? I do it all the time. When you do that, the browser displays a standard text field. Why? Fault tolerance! It doesn't know what an `input` of type "adio" is, so it falls back to the default `input` type: text.

This is yet another way the fault-tolerant nature of HTML enables the language to evolve. It's what allows you to use newer form controls such as "email" and "range" without making the form unusable to folks who are using browsers that don't understand those `input` types. It's pretty amazing.

---

38 The browser will also take into account a ton of other factors, as detailed in the spec at `https://perma.cc/B6YW-3YLR`.

Now here's the *coup de grâce*, courtesy of web developer Jeremy Keith:[39]

```
<label for="state" id="state_label">State</label>
<datalist id="states">
  <select name="state" aria-labelledby="state_label">
    <option>Alabama</option>
    <option>Alaska</option>
    <option>Arizona</option>
    <option>Arkansas</option>
    <!-- options continue -->
  </select>
  If other, please specify
</datalist>
<input id="state" name="state" list="states">
```

I'll give you a moment to look that over and come up with what the primary interaction is and what the fallback is.

(Yeah, I'm humming the *Jeopardy* theme in my head.)

Ready? This example makes use of the `datalist` element, which, in concert with the `list` attribute, enables native input suggestions in the browser (a.k.a. predictive typing). As **Figure 3.7** shows, browsers that don't support `datalist` will see the "State" `label`, the `select`, the text "If other, please specify," and the text field; browsers that support `datalist` will see the "State" `label` and the text field only because the `datalist` element is allowed to contain only `option` elements (which it cleverly plucks from within the `select`).

---

39 http://perma.cc/DS8S-C8L5

Figure 3.7 *Two interpretations of the same markup: a browser that understands* datalist *displays one thing (above) and a browser that doesn't displays something else (below).*

Mind blown? That's the power of fault tolerance.

MARKUP CONVEYS MEANING

Good user experience starts with content, but it is your job to do whatever you can to ensure the meaning of your words ring loud and clear. By being deliberate in choosing appropriate HTML elements and in providing fallbacks for older browsers when you use new ones, you ensure your users can actually *use* the markup you write. When you diligently police your markup for cruft and presentational tags, you keep your pages small and avoid confusing your users. When you add greater meaning and structure through microformats, microdata, and RDFa, you increase the potential reach of your content and make it more useful for your customers.

As this chapter has demonstrated, embracing the inherent awesomeness of HTML is not only easy, it also improves your users' experiences dramatically.

"I've been amazed at how often those outside the discipline of design assume that what designers do is decoration— likely because so much bad design simply is decoration. Good design isn't. Good design is problem solving."

—JEFFREY VEEN

CHAPTER 4:
VISUAL DESIGN IS AN ENHANCEMENT

In 2012, a blog post from Jason Samuels of NCFR (National Council on Family Relations) caught my eye.[1] In the post, Jason took a look at the analytics data collected from the NCFR site[2] over a four-year period to demonstrate how much the profile of its users—professionals studying family dynamics and such—had changed over that period.

He found that OS-wise, Windows use had dropped from 93.5 percent to 72.4 percent, no doubt because of the rise of Apple's OS X and iOS as well as Google's Android operating system. As you'd likely expect, he found that mobile usage (including tablets) had grown year over year at a rate of 200 to 400 percent from a paltry 0.1 percent in 2008 to 6.2 percent in 2012. Couple the decline of Windows with the rise of mobile and the launch of Chrome (which came out in 2008) and it's no wonder Jason also saw a sharp decline in Internet Explorer's numbers: Internet Explorer dropped from a dominant position, bringing 75.5 percent of their visits, to a mere 37 percent.

---

1   http://perma.cc/K75N-PFXN
2   http://perma.cc/Y8FQ-YCCS

These stats make complete sense if you were working on the Web at that time. Our relationship with the Web was changing just as new hardware and software options for accessing it were being rolled out. That said, nothing had quite prepared me for what he found regarding screen sizes: In 2008, he detected 71 different screen resolutions, but in the first quarter of 2012, he detected a whopping *830!*

Think about that for a minute: 830 different screen resolutions? That's astounding! But wait, there's more. Jason updated the post in 2014 to reflect stats from the first quarter of that year, when he was seeing an average of about 1,000 unique screen resolutions every quarter.

That stat blows my mind every time I read it. You can't create distinct layouts for 71 different screens, let alone 1,000. It's a fool's errand. And that's just variability in screen dimensions and says nothing about CSS capabilities, pixel density, and a host of other visual design–related concerns.

How do you manage all of these variables when it comes to visual design? You do what designers have been doing for centuries: You problem solve. You look for ways to do more with less. You embrace constraints and look for creative solutions to gnarly problems. If that sounds good to you, you're in the right place: The Web is full of gnarly problems and seemingly binding constraints.

Let's look at a few ways to tackle them, starting with how to make visual design work less complicated, more consistent, and incredibly flexible.

DESIGN SYSTEMS, NOT PAGES

In the early days of the Web, starting a new web design typically meant cracking open Adobe Photoshop and creating a new canvas onto which you'd draw a picture of a website. As browsers have provided more opportunities to write markup and CSS directly in the browser, some designers have begun to design there instead.

I'm not here to tell you which you should use; you should design wherever you feel most comfortable. You might even find you like to work in both.

What I am here to tell you, however, is that you should not be thinking about web design as page design. Web pages rarely exist in isolation, and when you go down the rabbit hole of designing a site in "pages," you run the risk of *overdesigning* it. I define overdesign as the practice of making every page type a one-off with only the most tacit aesthetic connections to its siblings within the site. I once worked on a project that had several designers who generated a staggering 135 unique page designs. That was overdesign. Madness, I tell you, madness.

Web developer Stephen Hay lays it out nicely in his book *Responsive Design Workflow.*

> *Think in terms of types. Think in terms of components. There are never many page types, so don't think too much about* pages. *One of my most challenging conversations with a client involved me explaining that I didn't have to redesign their site's 10,000 pages. Rather, we had to spend a lot of time analyzing their content, and then I would design about 10 or 12 pages (plus a battery of small components). I would be designing a* system. *Not individual pages.*

When you design systems, you create thematic links between elements and between pages. When you design systems, you inject predictability, which is comforting for your users. When you design systems, you make reuse easy, which is comforting for you as well.

The systems you design can be created in many ways, and the artifacts of these systems serve different purposes. I'll walk you through a few popular tools for designing systems and discuss how and when they can be useful.

Conduct a Design Audit

If you are redesigning an existing site, you should consider conducting a design audit.[3] With a design audit (or, as it's sometimes called, an *interface inventory*), you go page-by-page through your existing website (and the wireframes for the new one), collecting screenshots of each unique style element you spot: headings, buttons, icons, bullets, promotional blocks, and so on. You can do this pretty easily with screen-capture software like the one that's built into OS X or with programs like Skitch or Jing.[4]

A design audit is quite helpful for seeing how consistently the site's brand is realized. If the site in question has been up for quite some time, it's pretty likely that you will find elements that don't fit, either because the aesthetic of the organization shifted over time without all the assets being updated or because new designers came onto the project and wanted to do something different. The reasons why your site has 14 different button styles don't really matter, though—design consistency does. Design consistency belies reliability and trustworthiness. It makes your users feel more comfortable and secure.[5]

Design audits are also invaluable as you establish a visual language for your site. They remind you of all the elements you will need to design as part of your design system.

---

3   http://perma.cc/8BU5-BP6H

4   http://perma.cc/3W8V-RJ9Q

5   http://perma.cc/86A4-LT8V

Explore Visual Language with Style Tiles

During the ideation phase of your design process, you might consider using what designer Samantha Warren refers to as *style tiles*.[6] Style tiles are single-page documents that represent a design direction through a collection of interface elements such as headings, body copy, iconography, buttons, and whatever elements might be seminal to the purpose of the site (**Figure 4.1**).

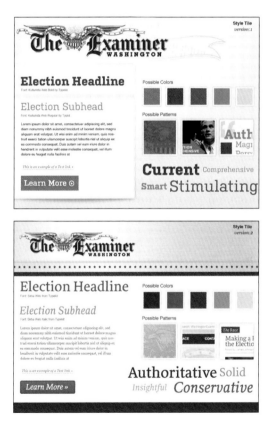

Figure 4.1 *Style tiles from Phase2 Technology's 2012 election site for the* Washington Examiner. *You can read the case study at* http://perma.cc/QW7M-YCTZ.

6   http://perma.cc/WT7D-9FC6

Style tiles allow you to focus on the overall theme for a site in isolation, and their simplicity means you can revise them easily (or produce a few alternates if you want to offer multiple design directions). You rarely see all the important components of a site on a single page, so style tiles let you look at the collection of interface elements at once, which helps you ensure they fit well together.

Create a Style Guide or a Pattern Library

When you design a system, you need to document that system somewhere. Two popular options for this kind of documentation are style guides and pattern libraries. The actual definitions of these artifacts of the design process seem to vary a little from company to company, but I will explain them in the way I hear them most commonly used (and how I use them in my own practice).[7]

Style guides came to us from the print design world, and they collect all the visual design assets that comprise a site. Taken together, they *are* the design. Think of them as exhaustive style tiles. Often style guides contain annotations about font sizes, spacing, margins, image sizes, ad dimensions, and the like. They may also indicate the purpose that each element serves, but that's not always the case. Style guides can exist as HTML documents, PDFs, JPEGs, or even printed books.

Pattern libraries are essentially living style guides. They don't often contain annotations (though they can), but they exist as live web documents. Pattern libraries should use the same HTML, CSS, and JavaScript that is or will be used on the live site. This can make a pattern library a bit more useful than a style guide (especially a

---

7   A word of warning: I have heard them used interchangeably, so if you aren't sure what someone is talking about when they say either of these terms—or something completely different that hints at a similar idea—it's best to ask for clarification. Teams need to speak the same language and have a shared understanding of what terms mean.

PDF one). Often pattern libraries even provide easy access to the HTML markup so front-end developers can grab that code and drop it into the templates they are assembling.

There are numerous tools for creating pattern libraries. Some popular ones include Barebones, Pattern Lab, Pattern Primer, and Style Prototype.[8] For small projects, a pattern library might be overkill, but for large projects, they are well worth the investment. They can take time to produce, but once you have established the design patterns, you've essentially created a bucket full of Lego-like pieces that can be fit together in scads of different ways to serve the purpose of every page on your site. Website production goes much more quickly when you have a pattern library.

Additionally, when you think about your design as a system of related components and maintain them within a pattern library, you can isolate each component to ensure it will adapt to your users' needs. This isolation is also incredibly helpful when it comes to testing your designs on real devices because you are able to limit the number of variables at play and focus on each component individually.

This isolation also allows you to focus on the purpose of every component and how that relates to your content. After all, you are designing a system in support of your content, not just for giggles.

---

8   An excellent roundup of pattern library generators is available at
     http://perma.cc/LK5K-6K8Z.

DON'T DESIGN YOURSELF INTO A CORNER

As I mentioned in Chapter 2, "final content" is always a challenge. It's an elusive beast that often takes time (and committees) to produce. The time required to create real content is often underestimated, causing project leadership to put pressure on you to just "get something going" in the design world. If you don't, the project might not get done on time. And it will be all your fault. *No pressure.*

As Jeff Veen astutely observed in the quote opening this chapter, design without purpose is not design—it's decoration. You need content to understand how you can help it become more lively, more effective, and more understandable. The purpose of design is to illuminate. It's your job, as designer, to push back against decoration and explain that design has a purpose, and it needs content to realize that purpose. Or you need to make things up.

Design the Conversation

In Chapter 2, I mentioned that—in the absence of final content—you might consider *borrowing* content from a competitor's site to help you think more clearly about the types of content you need in order to design your site, but there are many instances where borrowing representative content from other sites gets you only so far. Navigation, for instance. Button labels. Error messages. All these things need to be in your company's voice and appropriate to your audience. As a designer, you should be aware of the purpose of each page and should feel comfortable making suggestions about what those elements should read like. You can (and should) contribute to the conversation your interface is having.

If you don't do this and use only Lorem Ipsum in your designs, you run the risk of letting your design dictate your content rather than the other way around. When you are designing in Photoshop, in Sketch, or even in the browser, it's easy to shave off a few words (or paragraphs) here or there to tweak the proportions of the container block to look just right on top of an image. But that isn't grounded in reality.

You may find that the copy you end up getting is necessarily longer or shorter than what you planned for. That's when things get awkward. Do you cut or truncate the copy to make it fit? Do you add more content to fill the space? Either decision compromises the content and (possibly) the usability of your site (**Figure 4.2**). The other option is to change the design to accommodate the content (which is often the correct choice), but that will probably be painful too. How many rounds of revision did that design go through again?

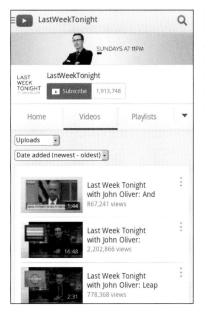

Figure 4.2 *YouTube designed the teaser blocks for videos to have only a certain amount of text. When the program name is long, users get no useful information in the teaser, as in this screenshot taken in Opera Mobile on an HTC Evo 4G.*

To avoid situations like this, it's crucial for content strategists, copywriters, and designers to all be on the same page. Designers need to have a good sense of anticipated content length and key words that might be particularly long. Content authors need to be aware of any design constraints they need to consider, such as character limits for buttons, headlines, and teasers. Working together will help establish a shared understanding of what the needs of the content are and ensure the pieces fit together well when the time comes.

Find the Edges

Content is the foundation of design. It's why you're building a website in the first place. It needs to be the starting point of your design work and needs to be central to every design decision you make.

When working with copy—real or representative or even Lorem Ipsum—we have a tendency to design for the ideal scenario. We use brief, punchy copy for product descriptions or terse calls to action for buttons and links. It's natural. It feels good. Sadly, that's not reality. When designing a given module, it's always good to throw something ugly in there that breaks from the norm, the comfortable.

Do your product descriptions typically have five bulleted features? Make sure the design holds up when you have one with two and another with 20.

Have nice content images where everyone in the photo is looking in the direction of the text? What if they are facing the other way, off the screen?[9] And speaking of photos, are all of your photos in the same aspect ratio? What if you have one that is overly wide or overly tall that doesn't fit quite right (**Figure 4.3**)? What if your call to action runs two lines instead of one? What if it runs three? What if your product title includes two really long words? What if the site is being translated into German?[10]

Considering the edge cases early on makes for more robust designs. It's kind of like how it's easier to put together a jigsaw puzzle once you've framed it out with the edge pieces.

---

9   Thankfully, we tend to face right most of the time in photos, so we're usually looking left on the page, but there's always an outlier (http://perma.cc/TAP6-AW8V).

10 A word of advice regarding horizontal navigation in German—don't do it.

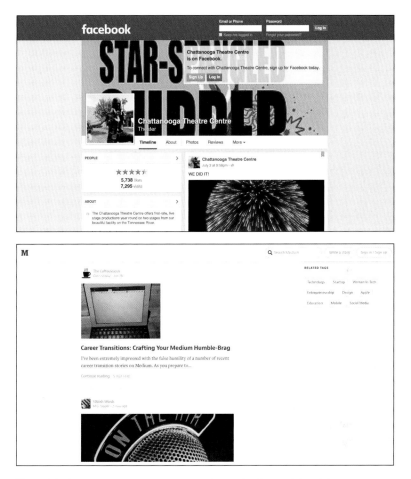

Figure 4.3 *The Chattanooga Theatre Centre's Facebook page (above) has a cover photo that is oriented vertically. Facebook scales it to fill the allotted space, but the result is pretty horrible. Whenever you are dealing with user-generated content, it pays to design defensively. Medium (below) handles user-uploaded images with different aspect ratios rather well.*

UNDERSTAND HOW CSS WORKS

This isn't a CSS book, so I'm not going to walk you through all the options available to you in CSS. One thing I do want to do, however, is give you an ever-so-brief recap of how CSS works because I think it will provide invaluable insight into how to construct progressive designs. If you're already an expert in CSS, this section may be a bit remedial, but I suggest you at least skim it. The principles of CSS I'll cover here are not often discussed, but understanding them will undoubtedly make you a better coder.

At its most fundamental, CSS is a series of human-readable rule sets, each composed of a selector and declaration block containing a set of property-value pairs (declarations) to be applied to any element matched by the selector.

```
p {
  color: red;
  font-weight: bold;
}
```

The previous example is about as basic as CSS gets. Anyone who's worked with CSS before (and probably even someone who hasn't) can look at it and quickly comprehend that it selects paragraphs and makes their text bold and red. Easy peasy.

Proximity Is Powerful

The first topic I want to discuss with you is the *cascade* (it is the first word in Cascading Style Sheets after all). The cascade is a pretty easy concept to understand: When everything else is equal, the last value defined for a given property wins. I'll come back to the "when everything else is equal" bit in a moment, but let's focus on that second half: The last value defined for a given property wins. This is sometimes referred to as the *proximity* aspect of the cascade. Here's an example:

```
p {
  color: red;
  color: green;
}
```

Now this isn't something you would typically do, but bear with me. When this CSS is applied to the page, the color of all paragraphs would be green rather than red because the "green" color declaration comes second. In other words, the "green" color value overwrites the "red" color value. Let's look at another example:

```
p {
  color: red;
}
/* imagine some more rule sets here */
p {
  color: green;
}
```

This example has two rule sets with identical selectors but different values assigned for color. This sort of thing happens a little more frequently, typically when you are working on large style sheets or on a team. As you'd expect, paragraphs will be green because the latter declaration wins. It's closer in proximity to the element it's affecting.

Expanding this a bit further, consider moving these rule sets into two separate embedded style sheets in the head of the document.

```
<style>
  p {
    color: red;
  }
</style>
<style>
  p {
    color: green;
  }
</style>
```

Still green. Move them to linked style sheets.

```
<link rel="stylesheet" href="red-paragraph.css">
<link rel="stylesheet" href="green-paragraph.css">
```

Still green. Each of these examples results in a green paragraph because of proximity—the color value was redefined from "red" to "green" in rules that came later in the document. Now here's a tricky one:

```
<style>
  p {
    color: green;
  }
</style>
<link rel="stylesheet" href="red-paragraph.css">
```

In this instance, you might think the paragraph would go red because the linked style sheet comes second, but that's not the case. Proximity has to do with the distance of the rule to the content in terms of position in the document, true, but it also has to do with actual distance of the rule from the element it describes, following the *cascade order*. It goes like this:

1. Browser default styles
2. Linked external style sheets (by order they're linked)
3. Embedded style sheets (by order they're embedded)
4. Inline styles (which I'll discuss in a second)

That means declarations in linked style sheets may be overridden by declarations in embedded style sheets. That's why the paragraphs would still be green.

At the end of the line are the inline styles.

```
<style>
  p {
    color: green;
  }
</style>
<link rel="stylesheet" href="red-paragraph.css">
```

```
<!-- more HTML -->

<p>This paragraph is green.</p>
<p style="color: blue">This paragraph is blue.</p>
```

As with the previous example, the style rule in the embedded style sheet would turn the first paragraph green, but the inline style declaration trumps both the linked and embedded rules. It's as close as you can get with respect to proximity.

Why does this matter? Knowing how proximity works allows you to wield it to your advantage when applying CSS. I'll get into some of that shortly, but first let's tackle the bit about the cascade I skipped: "when everything else is equal." The "everything else" is *specificity*.

Specificity Trumps Proximity

Specificity is another core concept in CSS. It's a measure of how many elements a given selector can select and is the only mechanism available for overruling proximity. Some selectors are more specific than other selectors. For example, an `id` selector (e.g., `#intro`) is infinitely more specific than a `class` selector (e.g., `.vcard`), which is, in turn, infinitely more specific than a type selector (e.g., `p`).[11]

The specificity of a given selector is calculated by adding the specificity of all its component parts. Let's take a look at an example:

```
figure figcaption {
  color: green;
}
figcaption {
  color: red;
}
```

---

11 If you don't quite grasp how specificity is calculated, be sure to check out Andy Clarke's "CSS Specificity Wars," `http://perma.cc/TQZ2-DJGX`.

Here are two rule sets that each target a figure caption (figcaption). The figcaption element is valid only within a figure, so both rules should select any figcaption on the page. Any figcaption on the page will be green—even though the second rule has greater proximity—because the specificity of the first selector is greater than that of the second. The first rule's selector includes two type selectors (figure and figcaption), which is more than the second rule's single type selector (figcaption).

If, however, you were to change things up and switch to using a class for the selector in the latter rule set, the results would be different.

```
figure figcaption {
  color: green;
}
.caption {
  color: red;
}
```

In this instance, the class selector (.caption) is more specific than the two type selectors combined. A good rule of thumb for figuring out which selectors are more specific is to assign a value to each component part of the selector:

- 0 to any universal selector (*)
- 1 to any type or pseudo-element selector (e.g., p or ::before)
- 10 to any class, pseudoclass, or attribute selector (e.g., .caption, :hover, or [alt])
- 100 to any id selector (e.g., #top)

If you use this formula, just be aware that 11 class selectors will never trump an id selector because each of these groupings is infinitely more specific than the ones in the grouping after them.

Rules applied via more specific selectors will trump those applied with less specific selectors, regardless of their order in the cascade.

Specificity of selectors is something that takes time to master and can cause any number of headaches. If you apply all your styles with heavy-handed selectors (e.g., each one contains an id selector), you end up having to create even more specific selectors to overrule them (e.g., two `id` selectors). To avoid an ever-escalating arms race of specificity, I recommend you make your selectors as nonspecific as possible.[12] In other words, keep things simple and work with your markup. Thoughtful, meaningful markup choices—the kind discussed in Chapter 3—should be your guide. Microformat `class` names and ARIA attributes can be particularly useful for keeping your selectors minimally specific.

Errors Create Opportunity

The final aspect of CSS I want to touch on is how fault tolerance applies to CSS. You'll remember from Chapter 1 that fault tolerance is the chief means by which CSS and HTML are empowered to evolve over time without sacrificing backward-compatibility. In both languages, it comes down to a single rule for browsers: Ignore what you don't understand.

In HTML, this means unknown elements and attributes are ignored and the browser moves on, but in CSS the error handling works a little differently.

When parsing CSS to determine how to render a page, a browser reads each rule set and examines it. If it encounters something it doesn't understand, it experiences something called a *parsing error*. Parsing errors aren't scary things. They don't often cause your site to fall apart like JavaScript program errors do. Parsing errors in CSS are fault tolerant in the same way HTML is fault tolerant. Though they are often the result of malformed CSS syntax (e.g., the misspelling of a property name or value, a missing colon or semicolon, etc.), they also result when perfectly valid CSS syntax is simply beyond the parser's comprehension. Let's revisit that simple rule set that kicked off this section.

---

12 Numerous style systems based on `class` selectors have taken off because of the challenges of specificity. BEM and SMACSS are two examples of this and can help you avoid writing overly specific selectors by relying on every element having a `class` (or two or three) assigned to it. This can make your CSS more modular but can bloat your HTML. *Trade-offs!*

```
p {
  color: red;
  font-weight: bold;
}
```

Assuming all the curly braces, colons, and semicolons are in their proper places (which they are), this example might not be interpreted the way you'd expect. According to the specification,[13] if a browser encounters this rule set and doesn't understand any part of it (i.e., it experiences a parsing error), the browser must ignore the larger component of the rule set in which the parsing error occurs.

So, for example, if the browser did not understand the CSS `color` keyword "red," it would ignore the declaration `color:  red` but would still apply the remaining declarations. The same goes for the `font-weight` keyword "bold." If, however, the browser was unable to understand the selector (`p`), it would ignore the entire rule set, regardless of the browser's ability to comprehend either of the declarations it contained.

The reasoning behind this is simple: We don't know what the future of CSS may be. As a language, CSS continues to evolve. New features are added, and, on occasion, older features may be removed. For websites to work properly and for CSS to be a reliable design language, it's imperative that a browser ignores declarations and selectors it doesn't recognize. This flexibility not only helps you avoid exposing errors to your users but makes it possible to progressively enhance pages using CSS.

Property Fallbacks

For properties, using parsing errors to your advantage is pretty straightforward, and it opens up some awesome possibilities. Here's a quick example using CSS3's RGBa color scheme:

---

13 http://perma.cc/RFC5-WHRC

```
p {
  background-color: rgb(137, 224, 160);
  background-color: rgba(180, 246, 248, .43);
}
```

A browser parsing this rule set would likely understand the selector (after all, you can't get much simpler than a type selector), so it would move on to the first `background-color` declaration. The `background-color` property has been part of CSS since version 1, so the browser should have no problem there and would move on to the assigned value. RGB-based color values have also been part of CSS since the beginning, so the browser will understand that value too. With the first declaration passing muster with the parser, the browser would apply `background-color: rgb(137, 224, 160)` to all paragraphs and then move on to the second declaration.

In the second declaration, `background-color` is redefined with a new value (overriding the previous declaration, per the cascade). Obviously, as I discussed, the browser understands the property, so it would move on to the declared value, which uses RGBa.[14] If the browser understands RGBa, there's no problem, and the RGBa value is assigned to the `background-color` property, overwriting the original RGB value. If RGBa is not supported, such as in the case of IE 8, the browser experiences a parsing error and ignores the entire declaration, leaving all paragraphs with the original RGB value for `background-color`.

This is a pretty simple example of how you can use CSS's fault-tolerant nature to deliver an enhanced experience to users on more modern browsers without sacrificing the experience of folks on older ones. This technique can be used for other values that have been introduced over time such as the `calc()` function, viewport units (vw and vh), and "flex." Following this approach ensures your design is robust and will work anywhere. It's pretty easy to do, too!

---

14 RGBa, in case you aren't familiar, is an RGB color with an alpha channel that governs opacity.

Hiding Rule Sets

Using parsing errors to your advantage doesn't just work at the declaration level, though; you can apply this same technique to hide entire rule sets from a particular browser by using a more advanced selector.

```
:matches(body) nav {
  /* A bunch of advanced stuff goes here */
}
```

Any browser encountering this rule set would parse it, starting with the selector. If the browser understands type selectors and the `:matches` pseudoclass, it will continue parsing the rule set and apply the declarations it understands. If, on the other hand, said browser does not comprehend any one of the selectors used, it would experience a parsing error and ignore the entire rule set.[15]

Perhaps the most famous example that uses this technique to selectively deliver rules to one browser over another (more for effect than practicality) is Egor Kloos' CSS Zen Garden entry titled "Gemination" (**Figure 4.4**). In this proof-of-concept piece, Kloos created a basic layout aimed at Internet Explorer (then in version 6) and employed a technique dubbed MOSe ("Mozilla/Opera/Safari enhancement")[16] to offer more advanced browsers a completely different experience. Kloos used simple selectors for the basic layout and advanced selectors for the enhanced styles. Here's a snippet that demonstrates his approach:

---

15 If you're interested, that selector finds any `nav` element that is a descendant of a `body` element, but it does so using a CSS4 selector.

16 Dave Shea, curator of the CSS Zen Garden, coined the term in 2003, but when Internet Explorer 7 came out, the term fell out of use because it didn't have the same selector-based limitations as IE 6. You can read his original post at `http://perma.cc/GQX7-DBJL`. Why not MOSCE, you ask? Chrome didn't exist yet.

Figure 4.4 *Egor Kloos'*
"Gemination"—
http://perma.cc/
GL2V-YPY8—*in IE 6*
(left) and IE 7 (top).

```
#intro {
  /* Basic styles for IE6 */
}

/* More styles here */

body[id=css-zen-garden] #intro {
  /* Advanced styles for everyone else */
}
```

Following CSS cascade order, the browser parses the first rule set first to render the #intro layout. A little later, the browser parses the "enhanced" rule set for #intro. If the browser understands attribute selectors, it will render a completely different layout for #intro; if it doesn't, it will ignore the new rule set entirely.

Selector-based screening can be a useful technique, but it tends to trip up many CSS authors who don't realize selector failure in a compound selector (two or more selector statements, separated by commas) is complete, not discrete.

```
p, p[class] {
  color: red;
  font-weight: bold;
}
```

This example has the same potential for parsing errors as the example that opened this chapter. Browsers that understand only one of the selectors in the compound selector will ignore the entire rule set rather than just the advanced selector (which, in case you were wondering, finds paragraphs with class attributes).

Though it may seem unintuitive, the CSS 2.1 spec clearly states that this is how it should be: "The whole statement should be ignored if there is an error anywhere in the selector, even though the rest of the selector may look reasonable."[17] Every CSS rule set has only one selector. The commas act as an "or" separating multiple options, but those options are not distinct when it comes to parsing.

Knowing this, you can make better decisions about how and when to combine selectors. As a general rule, it's best to avoid combining advanced selectors with simple ones (as in the example) unless you want to hide the whole rule set from older browsers.

Hiding Multiple Rule Sets

From a maintainability standpoint, this method is not ideal for more than a single rule set here and there; to apply the concept of rule set filtering en masse, you can use *at-rules*.

```
@media screen {
  p {
    color: red;
  }
}

@media only screen {
  p {
    color: green;
  }
}
```

In this example, all browsers that support the "screen" media type will turn the text of paragraphs red. Only browsers that support media queries (signified by the "only" keyword) will turn their paragraph text green. In other words, browsers will not apply rule sets that appear within at-rules they can't comprehend. The same logic applies with other at-rule blocks such as @supports (which I'll talk about shortly).

---

17 http://perma.cc/VS5C-AD4F

It's worth noting, however, that some at-rules allow for compound assignment using a comma, like you do in selectors. The behavior is a little different, however.

```
@media screen, print, refrigerator {
  p {
    color: green;
  }
}
```

A browser that encounters this at-rule will turn paragraphs green in whichever media they can match (i.e., screen and print because I made the refrigerator media type up). In other words, compound media assignment *does not* work like compound selectors: An unknown statement within a compound selector will cause the browser to ignore *the whole rule set*, but an unknown value member within a recognized compound at-rule will cause the browser to ignore only *the unrecognized at-rule value*.

Example: Progressive Navigation

In Chapter 3, I mentioned that Nichols College had an interesting approach to handling its mobile navigation where the links are at the end of the document and there is a "jump" link that anchors you down to them and another that takes you from the navigation back to the content. Here's an excerpt of the markup from the Graduate & Professional Studies site:[18]

```
<header id="top">
  <!-- logo, etc. -->
  <p id="jump">
    <a href="#nav"><b>Jump to the Navigation
    </b>Menu</a>
  </p>
</header>
```

---

18 http://perma.cc/42JU-T7DE

```
<!-- content, content, content... -->

<nav role="navigation">
  <ul id="nav" tabindex="-1">
    <!-- navigation options -->
    <li id="back"><a href="#top">Back to
    top</a></li>
  </ul>
  <!-- search form -->
</nav>

<!-- footer, etc. -->
```

The baseline experience of the navigation is the same as what you saw in Chapter 3 with *Contents Magazine*: The user clicks the "jump" link and the browser scrolls to the navigation. The user clicks the "back" link and the browser goes back to the top of the page. It's not terribly elegant, but it works everywhere (even without CSS).

With CSS, the links are designed to be easily tappable with your fingers on a small touchscreen (**Figure 4.5**). That's a nice affordance for browsers with only basic CSS support. Browsers with more advanced CSS support, however, receive a much more elegant solution: Tapping the jump link reveals the navigation right beneath the site header (**Figure 4.6**).

Figure 4.5. *A selection of the Nichols College Graduate & Professional Studies site navigation in Opera Mobile on an HTC Hero. Note that the links are easy to tap.*

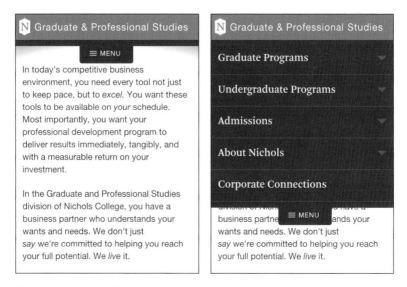

Figure 4.6. *Nichols College Graduate & Professional Studies' enhanced site navigation collapsed (left) and expanded (right). View the video of it in action at* http://perma.cc/KP9B-K6PM.

The site achieves this using the :target pseudoclass, which selects any element whose id matches the fragment identifier in the URL. First, the developers positioned the list just below the header using absolute positioning. Then, they set up the default styles for when the navigation (ul#nav) is not targeted, giving the list items a height of 0. When the navigation is targeted (which happens when the "jump" link is tapped), the list items return to their normal height. Here's an excerpt of the CSS that makes it possible:

```
#nav li {
  height: 0;
  overflow: hidden;
}
#nav:target li {
  height: auto;
}
```

Some browsers (IE 8, for instance) don't support `:target`, so Nichols uses a CSS-based filter—`body:not(:target)`—to restrict these rules to only browsers that understand the `:target` pseudoclass. They added that selector as a prefix to any selectors in the rule sets that govern this enhancement. So, the rules actually look like this:

```
body:not(:target) #nav li {
  height: 0;
  overflow: hidden;
}
body:not(:target) #nav:target li {
  height: auto;
}
```

Taking this step ensures that older browsers remain able to access the navigation in the default manner (at the bottom of the page). Without the filter in there, those browsers would never see the navigation because the default state was for the list items to be hidden.

In another clever application of CSS, Nichols College uses the "back" link as a hidden layer to trigger the menu to be collapsed (because when you click it, `#nav` is no longer targeted). The developers absolutely position the layer and set its left and right offsets to 0 and set absurdly large negative top and bottom offsets to make it cover the page. They then place the main navigation links on top of it in the stacking order using `z-index` (**Figure 4.7**).

Here's the code that handles that:

```
body:not(:target) #nav li a {
  position: relative;
  z-index: 1;
}
#nav:target #back a {
  position: absolute;
  left: 0;
  right: 0;
```

```
  top: -999em;
  bottom: -99em;
  z-index: 0;
}
```

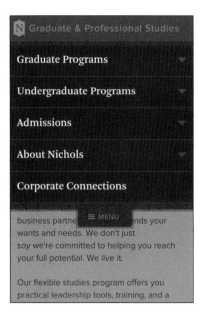

Figure 4.7. *Nichols College's exposed navigation with the "back" link highlighted in red (it's transparent by default.)*

As if that wasn't enough, Nichols College makes use of the `transition` property to animate the height change for the navigation list items. It gives the whole thing a "JavaScript-y" feel (even though no JavaScript is involved).

```
body:not(:target) #nav li a {
  transition: height .25s linear;
}
```

Since this approach to navigation works best on narrower screens, Nichols College uses a different layout when the screen size gets large enough to accommodate a horizontal nav (which they move from the bottom of the page to the top using absolute positioning). To sequester these styles to smaller screens only—so they don't have to override all these styles when they build the horizontal nav—the developers use a `max-width` media query.

```
@media (max-width: 59.9375em) {
   /* All of the mobile navigation-related styles */
}
```

Interestingly, that media query is contained within a linked style sheet with its own media query.

```
<link rel="stylesheet" href="/c/layouts.css"
      media="only screen and (min-width:20em)">
```

Taken together, the `link` and `@media` block ensure these styles apply only in media query–aware browsers that have a screen size of between 20em and just shy of 60em. This is an excellent example of progressive enhancement that takes full advantage of parsing errors to selectively deliver the enhanced experience to only those users who can actually benefit from it. Clearly, knowing how these mechanisms work pays huge dividends when you start considering browser and device proliferation.

START SMALL AND BE RESPONSIVE

In 2010, web designer Ethan Marcotte was seeking an elegant way to address device proliferation and the requests he was getting from clients.

In recent years, I've been meeting with more companies that request 'an iPhone website' as part of their project. It's an interesting phrase: At face value, of course, it speaks to mobile WebKit's quality as a browser, as well as a powerful business case for thinking beyond the desktop. But as designers, I think we often take comfort in such explicit requirements, as they allow us to compartmentalize the problems before us. We can quarantine the mobile experience on separate subdomains, spaces distinct and separate from 'the non-iPhone website.' But what's next? An iPad website? An N90 website? Can we really continue to commit to supporting each new user agent with its own bespoke experience? At some point, this starts to feel like a zero sum game. But how can we—and our designs—adapt?

In answering that question, Ethan came up with the design approach he termed *responsive web design*. This quote comes from his *A List Apart* article that introduced that concept.[19] Responsive web design came about as a way of addressing the varied screen sizes we were seeing back then (which pales in comparison to what we are seeing today).

Ethan came up with a basic formula—fluid grids, flexible media, and media queries—that allows a designer to control the visual design of a site across a wide swath of dimensions with little effort. Here's a breakdown:

1. **Fluid grids** (i.e., grid columns that are based on percentages) enable the layout to flex and fill the available space, making the layout adapt nicely to different widths.
2. **Flexible media** are images, videos, and the like that are not allowed to overflow their containers (typically, by setting a `width` or `max-width` of 100 percent on the associated element).
3. **Media queries** are then used to tweak the fluid grid to provide the most appropriate reading experience at that size by optimizing line lengths, font sizes, and so on.

In his original article, Ethan used two different kinds of media queries to adapt the layout of his demo page: `max-width` and `min-width`.[20]

```
/* CSS for the happy medium */

@media (max-width: 600px) {
  /* Adjustments for small screens */
}

@media (max-width: 400px) {
  /* Adjustments for even smaller screens */
}
```

---

19 http://perma.cc/3KR4-TA3J. He later wrote a book by the same name.
20 http://perma.cc/98PG-VF9Q

```
@media (min-width: 1300px) {
  /* Adjustments for larger screens  */
}
```

The `max-width` media query (`max-width: 600px`) is the CSS equivalent of saying *if the browser's width is less than or equal to 600px, apply these style rules.* The `min-width` media query (`min-width: 1300px`) says the opposite: *If the browser's width is greater than or equal to 1300px, apply these style rules.*

Both of these approaches are completely valid, but, a short while later, it was generally agreed that `min-width` media queries are the better way to go for your overall design because they are more efficient. They are more efficient because you end up writing less CSS when you are starting with a baseline and building up the design because you have more screen real estate. With the other approach, you end up writing a bunch of style rules for your large screen layout that you then have to override in order to apply the narrower design.

Let's look at a quick example to demonstrate the difference. Consider the following markup:

```
<div class="primary"></div>
<div class="secondary"></div>
```

Let's say I wanted the two `div` elements to stack on top of one another on a small screen but to sit side by side on a wider screen. If I consider the small screen first, I could simply say the following:

```
@media (min-width:600px) {
  .primary {
    float: left;
    width: 68%;
  }
  .secondary {
    float: right;
    width: 32%;
  }
}
```

This approach is sometimes referred to as *mobile first*, though with the advent of smart watches and other similarly tiny screens (that aren't necessarily *mobile*), I prefer the broader term *small screen first*. By contrast, if I wanted to get the same result but considered the large screen first—formerly *desktop first*—I would have to write this:

```
.primary {
  float: left;
  width: 68%;
}
.secondary {
  float: right;
  width: 32%;
}

@media (max-width:599px) {
  .primary, .secondary {
    float: none;
    width: auto;
  }
}
```

In other words, I would need to include two additional lines of CSS just to override the default settings outside of the media query. Those are unnecessary if I consider the small screen first because they come for free as part of the default rendering of a div element. In other words, approaching CSS thinking of the small screen first embraces default styles and progressively enhances the design when you have more screen real estate to work with.[21]

---

21 You can dissect these two contrasting approaches more on CodePen at http://perma.cc/G3KB-XXRC and http://perma.cc/79CZ-WEQ7.

Support Everyone, Optimize for Some

Understanding how browsers handle parsing errors makes it quite easy to draw a line in the sand between older, less capable browsers and modern ones. For example, you can divide your styles into basic styles that every browser can understand (e.g., typography, color, and margins) and more advanced styles that only modern browsers will be able to handle (e.g., layout, positioning, flexbox).

```
<link rel="stylesheet" href="basic.css" media="all">
<link rel="stylesheet" href="advanced.css"
      media="only screen">
```

Browsers that don't understand media queries[22] would download only the first style sheet. The "only" keyword was introduced with media queries and older browsers don't know what to make of it, so they ignore the style sheet. Modern browsers would download both. This approach is a perfect example of "mobile first" thinking because older mobile devices (which don't understand media queries) are not penalized by having to download a ton of styles they'll never use. It's a great use of media queries that works because, as web developer Bryan Rieger put it, "[T]he absence of support for @media queries is in fact the first @media query."[23]

It's worth noting that even older browsers like IE 8 are pretty good at handling floats and positioning. That said, IE 8 is a pretty old browser—it doesn't support media queries, flexbox layouts, or even RGBa. You might consider demoting your support for IE 8. I'm not saying to stop supporting IE 8 entirely, but you can give it a simpler experience. Taking the approach outlined earlier, you could use its lack of media query support to deliver it the mobile experience, and that would be okay. As long as users on IE 8 can still do what they need to do, they don't need to have the same visual design as someone on the latest version of Chrome, Edge, Firefox, Opera, or Safari.

---

22 http://perma.cc/RK52-VRZN
23 http://perma.cc/G63F-EYT4

Now, you might think that delivering a minimally designed website would annoy any users getting that experience. That's not necessarily the case. If the experience on that device was not so great previously, it might be a pleasant surprise. One of my favorite examples of this comes from *A List Apart*. In 2001, it stopped delivering CSS to Netscape Navigator 4 and other 4.0 generation browsers. Here's what the magazine's cofounder (and web standards luminary) Jeffrey Zeldman had to say about it at the time:

> *We assume that those who choose to keep using 4.0 browsers have reasons for doing so; we also assume that most of those folks don't really care about "design issues." They just want information, and with this approach they can still get the information they seek. In fact, since we began hiding the design from non–compliant browsers in February 2001, ALA's Netscape 4 readership has increased, from about 6% to about 11%.*[24]

That's right: When *A List Apart* switched from delivering a design to Netscape Navigator 4 to delivering only the content, it actually saw the use of that browser *increase*. In other words, the magazine delivered a better, more appropriate experience in that browser, and people appreciated it.

We often look at usage stats for our sites and take them at face value. One such example of this is seeing a low percentage of a particular browser, say, 0.1 percent. You might look at a paltry number like that and reason that it's not worth testing or even considering that browser. Before jumping to conclusions like this, however, you should look at these percentages in light of your actual usage numbers—0.1 percent of 1,000 visitors (i.e., one person) is different than 0.1 percent of 1,000,000 users (i.e., 1,000 people).

It's also worth questioning why the usage stats for that particular browser might be low. Start by looking at your site in that browser. How's the experience? If the experience is a good one, then it's likely nothing you've done has unintentionally skewed that number.

---

24 http://perma.cc/J8SD-QCZS

If it's not a good experience, however, then you might be artificially depressing usage of that browser by prohibiting folks from accomplishing what they need to on that browser. You might want to look into addressing the issues you see, or, if it's easier, you might consider reducing the amount and type of content you are sending to that browser, just like *A List Apart* did.

Think of it this way: There's no musical listening experience quite like sitting dead-center in an acoustically perfect concert hall. A 7.1 channel stereo at home is not nearly the same but still offers a great experience. A 5.1 channel system isn't quite as impressive as 7.1 channels, but it's still better than basic two-channel stereo. And finally, there's mono—it's not even close to the same experience as a concert hall, but at least you're still listening to music.

The "mono" design is your baseline small-screen experience that will work on older browsers, desktop or otherwise (e.g., the stuff that can go in `basic.css`, as mentioned earlier). In all likelihood, the design will be linear (single column, vertically oriented). That works well for old browsers and narrow ones alike.

Example: Growing a Layout

When you think about layout from a mobile-first perspective, you need to begin with optimizing things for as narrow a screen as best you can. Perhaps that screen size is 240px wide, like some feature phones, or even 144px, like some smart watches. Regardless, in addressing a small screen, you'll want to maximize your use of space. At the same time, however, you also want to keep text from crashing awkwardly into the side of the screen. The *Boston Globe*[25] achieves this balance by letting its primary layout elements maintain their default width while the primary content block (`div#main`) has a 10px margin on the left and right (**Figure 4.8**).

---

25 http://perma.cc/H2QN-BMJ6

Figure 4.8 *The* Boston Globe *website on a narrow screen with the margins of the primary content* div *highlighted using the Chrome browser's Developer Tools.*

On browsers with a little more horizontal space, the website still maintains a narrow margin, even though it has adjusted the layout to occupy two columns to make the most optimal use of space (**Figure 4.9**).

As the browser width increases, the website relaxes the layout a bit and increases the horizontal margins. It does this by removing the margin from the primary content div and setting the width of its parent container (div#contain) to 93.75 percent. It also centers the layout by defining a maximum width for div#contain so that it will never exceed 1232px and lets the browser autocalculate its horizontal margins (**Figure 4.10**). It does this all inside a media query that tests for a minimum width of 620px.

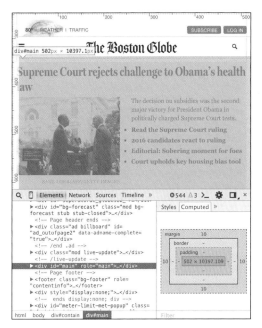

Figure 4.9 *The* Boston Globe *website on a wider screen maintains the same margins even though the layout is slightly different.*

Figure 4.10 *The widest version of the* Boston Globe *website.*

```
@media screen and (min-width: 620px) {
  #contain {
    margin: 0 auto 10px;
    width: 93.75%;
    max-width: 1232px;
  }
}
```

The design continues to adjust, keeping readable line lengths and making the most of the available space until it reaches that maximum with of 1232px—the "concert hall" experience, to bring back that analogy. The layout of the large screen page is far more complex than that of the small screen one, but the site works no matter how much screen real estate a user has available for it.

The *Boston Globe* web team's approach of delivering styles in this way had an unintended side effect: On a lark, designer Grant Hutchinson loaded the *Boston Globe* site on an Apple MessagePad 2100—an old PDA from 1997—and the site worked because progressive enhancement *just works* (**Figure 4.11**).

Figure 4.11 *The* Boston Globe *as viewed on in the Newt's Cape browser on an Apple MessagePad 2100. Screenshot by Grant Hutchinson, used with permission.*

The *Boston Globe* site is a perfect example of progressive enhancement with responsive web design. It's also great for another reason: The dimensions it chose for the media queries (a.k.a. breakpoints) don't directly map to any specific devices.

Embrace Fluidity

When we first began to address device proliferation with media queries, we started by mapping our media queries directly to common device dimensions (like those of the iPhone). Using media queries, it's entirely possible to get super-granular in an attempt to deliver certain rules only to particular devices.

Take a look at this beast:

```
@media only screen and (min-device-width:1024px)
                  and (max-width:989px),
      only screen and (max-device-width:480px),
      only screen and (max-device-width:480px)
                  and (orientation:landscape),
      only screen and (min-device-width:481px)
                  and (orientation:portrait) {
  /* Yikes! */
}
```

Now banish it from your mind and commit to never, ever writing something this heinous.[26]

I'm thankful that we now have a much better understanding of what we should and should not do with media queries and picking our breakpoints. Stephen Hay sums up the process for picking breakpoints beautifully.

> *Start with the small screen first, then expand until it looks like shit.* ***Time for a breakpoint!***

---

26 I will admit to writing this. I was young, and I needed the money.

What Stephen is saying here is simple: Let the content guide you. Start with your browser window very narrow and slowly make it wider. When the design starts to look awkward, it's probably time to insert a breakpoint to adjust the layout or the page or at least the given component.

Notice that Stephen never said anything about a specific device or browser. Every device is different, and while there are some common sizes, catering only to them can result in a poor experience for anyone who doesn't use one of those devices. Remember Jason Samuels and the 1,000 different screen sizes he was seeing every quarter? You can't design every one of those experiences. Chasing screen sizes is pointless. Instead, follow Stephen's advice and focus on the content. Let it be your guide and inform you as to where you need to add breakpoints.

Interestingly, Pattern Lab (which I mentioned earlier in this chapter) reinforces the idea that screen sizes vary widely. It has buttons to toggle the viewport to be "small," "medium," and so on, but the actual width varies each time you click one of them. In one instance, "small" might be 315px; in another it might be 345px. Pattern Lab also sports "Hay Mode," which starts the viewport off small and slowly enlarges it automatically, just as Stephen recommends (minus the swearing), and "Disco Mode," which randomly switches viewport sizes in order to stress test the design and makes it look like the browser is dancing.

When considering how your design plays out on different devices, it's still important to pay particular attention to certain, specific devices. That may sound contradictory to the universal support I've been advocating, but it's not. Certain devices are necessarily more important than others. For instance:

- Devices that frequently visit your site
- Devices that are used by your high-profile clients or the ones you want to attract
- Devices that are starting to take off in the marketplace

Ignoring devices that are used by a large percentage of your users (or by your most influential users) would be foolish. Optimizing the experiences for these devices is a good idea. Give them the "concert hall" experience; just don't forget about the long tail of other devices and browsers your users rely on to access your website. Support the long tail, but optimize for an important subset.

Everyone deserves to have their device supported, even if they get only the "mono" experience. The more people you support, the greater your reach and the more opportunity you create for sales, leads, visits, shares, or whatever other metrics you use to gauge your website's success.

FOCUS ON STANDARDS

Earlier on, in my examination of Nichols College's navigation, I showed the `transition` property. If you don't remember, here's the code again:

```
body:not(:target) #nav li a {
   transition: height .25s linear;
}
```

CSS transitions are part of CSS3 that was tested—during its development as a feature—on the open Web using vendor prefixes. You may have seen a vendor prefix before; `-webkit-` is probably the most common.

Vendor prefixes were created as a mechanism that would allow a browser maker (a.k.a. a vendor) to implement an experimental spec to let web designers "road test" the feature. The prefix indicates that the feature is experimental and may change in a future release. In other words, use at your own risk. Sadly, browsers often weren't very forthcoming about the experimental nature of these features and so we went ahead and used them in production on high-profile sites, often without providing a declaration that would support the future nonprefixed standard.

A perfect example of this becoming problematic is with CSS gradients. CSS gradients were introduced by WebKit in 2008 with a vendor prefix.[27] In the blog post unveiling this feature, Apple's Safari and WebKit Architect Dave Hyatt didn't explicitly state that this was an experiment, despite using the vendor prefix. Perhaps he assumed that was understood. This was an instance where Apple was testing the waters with an idea—CSS gradients didn't even make it into a Working Draft at the W3C for another three years.[28] Here's an example of the syntax from that post:

```
background: -webkit-gradient(
  linear, left top, left bottom,
  from(rgb(0, 171, 235)), to(rgb(255, 255, 255)),
  color-stop(0.5, rgb(255, 255, 255)),
  color-stop(0.5, rgb(102, 204, 0))
);
```

The syntax was pretty impenetrable, but designers were eager to make use of this new feature. After all, it allowed them to generate simple gradient images in the browser rather than having to download an additional asset. And so `-webkit-linear-gradient` migrated on to the Web and proliferated.

As it made its way through the standards process at the W3C, the syntax changed a bit from Apple's original proposal.[29] Other browsers picked up the revised syntax (as did Apple) and implemented it behind their own prefixes until the spec was deemed final.

As more browsers supported the feature, tools cropped up to enable you to generate the rather verbose gradient syntax; ColorZilla's tool[30] is particularly popular. To ensure all browsers that supported gradients were accommodated, you needed to write something akin to the following:

---

27 http://perma.cc/E8WD-AA7G

28 http://perma.cc/LS4C-JM96

29 http://perma.cc/Z8CL-DGWV

30 http://perma.cc/E2YS-9KES

```
background: #87e0fd;
background: -moz-linear-gradient(#87e0fd 0%,
            #0599c6 100%);
background: -webkit-gradient(linear, left top,
            left bottom,
            color-stop(0%,#87e0fd),
            color-stop(100%,#0599c6));
background: -webkit-linear-gradient(#87e0fd 0%,
            #0599c6 100%);
background: -o-linear-gradient(#87e0fd 0%,
            #0599c6 100%);
background: -ms-linear-gradient(#87e0fd 0%,
            #0599c6 100%);
background: linear-gradient(#87e0fd 0%,
            #0599c6 100%);
```

Background-by-background, these are the steps:

1. A solid color for older browsers
2. The vendor-prefixed Firefox version
3. The first pass from Apple, vendor-prefixed for WebKit (early Chrome used this syntax too)
4. The revised vendor-prefixed WebKit version
5. The vendor-prefixed Opera version
6. The vendor-prefixed IE version (supported in IE 10)
7. The official, standardized W3C version

As you'll recall, parsing errors results in an unknown value being ignored, so the order of these properties matters. It needed to be the default value first, the vendor prefixes in the middle, and the standardized version at the end. That way, when CSS gradients got standardized—which they were in 2012—the official version would always trump the vendor-prefixed versions.

Despite plenty of articles, blog posts, and examples demonstrating this syntax in order to reach the largest possible number of designers, sites were still being created using only the original concept from Apple. For example, up until its 2014 redesign, Macy's mobile site[31] used only the old linear gradient syntax in its navigation buttons (which were also `div` elements, not actual links, but I digress).

They were not the only ones to do this, of course; many other popular sites had and continue to have the same issue. This causes problems from an interoperability standpoint. For instance, without the gradient background, it's possible that the text could be unreadable (which wasn't the case with Macy's but could potentially be an issue on other sites).

To ensure users on other browsers got the experience designers intended, other browser makers eventually ended up having to support Apple's original experimental syntax, prefix and all.[32] Having to make an accommodation like this adds unnecessary bloat to a browser, making it larger and slower.

Having learned from this experience, most browser vendors have moved to put experimental features behind "flags" in the browser's configuration. To turn on an experimental feature, a user (or developer) would have to opt into it specifically. This should help reduce the likelihood of a situation like this arising in the future, but it's not a guarantee. It's possible that you could flip on the feature on your browser and forget that you've done so, giving you a false impression of something working for other users. I know; I've done it.

When it comes to features like this, it's important that you take note of their experimental nature. Don't rely on their availability unless you have some way of testing for whether they are supported (more on that in a minute). And if you do use a vendor-prefixed property, make sure you keep your style sheets updated as the spec for that property matures and as more browser vendors begin to implement it.

---

31 http://perma.cc/XD2R-BDKF. An archive of the version I'm referring to is available at http://perma.cc/4M7N-9Q5U.

32 http://perma.cc/A5WL-U5HY

If you use a CSS preprocessor like Sass, Less, or Stylus,[33] you may find that the preprocessor makes it easy to write the syntax according to the spec, and it will create the fallback and vendor-prefixed versions for you. Autoprefixer, a post-processor for CSS, will also take the W3C syntax for certain features and copy it to the vendor-prefixed versions based on the configuration you supply.[34]

DESIGN DEFENSIVELY

As I've mentioned a few times in this chapter, when you use new CSS features like gradients, you need to make sure you also provide an experience that works for users who don't have the ability to use that feature. You need to design defensively and provide fallbacks. Thankfully, that is pretty easy to do when you understand how fault tolerance works.

```
property: basic value;
property: advanced value;
```

Newer CSS properties and values will be ignored automatically because the browser knows to ignore anything it doesn't understand. If you have a bunch of advanced properties on an element and need to hide a whole CSS rule set, you can use a more advanced selector like you saw with the Nichols College navigation example. And if you want to hide several rule sets, you can use at-rules (including media queries) to achieve that too.

It's particularly important that you pay attention to color when it comes to devising different experiences for different browser generations. For instance, if you are using an RGBa color for a background, make sure the foreground color will still be legible

---

33 CSS preprocessors are beyond the scope of this book but might be useful in your workflow. Sass (http://perma.cc/4NH9-K8A3) is probably the most popular, with Less (http://perma.cc/9M5Y-FY6K) a close second. Stylus (http://perma.cc/XWK7-HA4N) is a distant third.

34 You can find a great introduction to Autoprefixer on CSS Tricks: http://perma.cc/SPF4-7PE8.

against your fallback. You can always supply two different fore-ground colors for each version if you need to by using the RGBa syntax (even if you are using an opaque color).

```
color: #fff;
color: rgba(29, 31, 33, 1);
background-color: #000;
background-color: rgba(255, 255, 255, 0.75);
```

In this example, the second `color` value is actually an opaque color but will be understood only by browsers that support RGBa, ensuring it partners well with the RGBa `background-color` value.

Be Conservative in How You Apply Styles

Sometimes you need more robust feature detection in order to isolate CSS code that could cause the design to fall apart in older browsers. Modernizr[35] has filled this need for many designers but relies on JavaScript to work. Since JavaScript is not always available, the W3C has introduced feature queries to allow you to achieve this kind of isolation. In practice, they work via a new at-rule: `@supports`.

Like the `@media` block for media queries, the `@supports` block acts as a wrapper around a collection of rule sets to enable you to selectively apply them only if your query evaluates as true. Queries can be made for a property or a property-value pair, and, as with `@media` blocks, you can also check for lack of support using the "not" keyword. Here are a few examples:

```
@supports (display:grid) {
  /* rule sets that would render the interface
     unusable without grid layout support */
}
```

---

35 http://perma.cc/BF8D-RS5S

```
@supports not (display:grid) or (display:-ms-grid) {
  /* Rules for browsers that don't support CSS Grid
     Layout */
}
```

It's worth noting that, as of this writing, `@supports` is still quite new, but it is—*er*—supported in more browsers with each new release.[36] The positive test case (example 1) is your best option; forward-compatibility is far more useful because only advanced browsers currently understand `@supports`. Older browsers will simply ignore it, making backward compatibility not quite as useful. However, as with media queries, lack of feature query support is, in fact, the first feature query.

Regardless, native CSS-based feature detection is an amazing tool for progressive enhancement. It allows better encapsulation and more granular testing without having to rely on JavaScript.

HIDE CONTENT RESPONSIBLY

Perhaps the most heavily repeated pattern in JavaScript-based interfaces is showing and hiding content. You've seen numerous examples that use it already: tabbed interfaces, accordions, and navigation. It crops up nearly everywhere.

In and of itself, this pattern is not a bad thing, but few people realize how profoundly your choice of hiding mechanism can influence the accessibility of your content when it comes to assistive technologies such as screen readers. It's important to know what the different approaches do and how they can affect the reading experience of your users.

---

36 Reference Can I Use for an updated support table:
    `http://perma.cc/QQB3-QLU4`.

Techniques to Avoid

Assuming you want your content available to screen readers, it's best to avoid using any of the following techniques to hide content.

Invisible

```
.hidden {
  visibility: hidden;
}
```

When you adjust the visibility of an element, the element is hidden from view but is not removed from the normal flow (i.e., it still takes up the space it normally would). Unfortunately, "black hat" SEO folks ruined this option when they started filling pages with popular keywords and hid them from view using this CSS property. To save screen-reader users from having to hear Pamela Anderson's name over and over,[37] assistive technology doesn't expose content hidden in this way.

Not Displayed

```
.hidden {
  display: none;
}
```

This is probably the most popular way of hiding content with CSS. Pretty much every JavaScript library does this by default. When you set `display` to `none`, the element is removed from the normal flow and hidden. The space it once occupied is collapsed. This was another technique used to "keyword stuff" pages so its contents are ignored by assistive technologies.

---

37 http://perma.cc/9CKZ-2Q3N

Collapsed

```
.hidden {
  height: 0;
  width: 0;
  overflow: hidden;
}
```

This setup collapses the element to nothing and prohibits its contents from flowing outside of its edges. This is yet another technique abused by the black hats, so it's not accessible. *People ruin everything!*

Techniques to Use Sparingly

These hiding techniques keep text accessible, but have some limitations.

Negatively Indented

```
.hidden {
  text-indent: -999em;
}
```

Finally, a technique that assistive technology does expose to users! The negative `text-indent` shifts the element's contents off-screen and out of view. Sadly, it works only with text and inline content, and links within the content may focus oddly. Also, you can never be sure the negative indent will be long enough to fully hide the content.

Positively Indented

```
.hidden {
  overflow: hidden;
  text-indent: 100%;
  white-space: nowrap;
  width: 20px; /* fixed width */
}
```

As with the previous example, this one is accessible. It's also limited to text and inline content. This approach is useful only when you know the precise width of the element.

Positioned Offscreen

```
.hidden {
  position: absolute;
  left: -999em;
}
```

A perennial favorite, this approach removes the content from the normal flow and shifts it off the left edge. The space the element occupied is collapsed. Its contents are accessible, but this approach works only in left-to-right languages. For right-to-left languages, use the `right` offset instead of `left`.

The Best Way to Go

Developed by a team at Yahoo!, this is the current gold standard for hiding content:

```
.hidden {
  position: absolute;
  height: 1px;
  width: 1px;
  overflow: hidden;
  clip: rect(1px, 1px, 1px, 1px);
}
```

It's a bit to take in, so I'll walk you through it.

The positioning removes the element from the normal flow, but because no offsets are used, it remains in its original position. The width and height collapse the element to a 1×1 square (which avoids the accessibility issues introduced by the 0×0 approach). Finally, its contents are hidden from view via a combination of `overflow` and `clip`. Using this technique, the element's content is accessible, and its text direction is irrelevant.

One thing to keep in mind with respect to hiding content is that when you hide elements such as images—which can have a significant effect on the performance of your page—in many cases the browser will still download the image.[38] Any users who don't get to see the hidden image are paying to get it and waiting to download it. The current best practice for selectively delivering images and other weighty assets is to load them via JavaScript, assuming, of course, they actually add to the experience (as we discussed in Chapter 2).

THE FLIP SIDE: GENERATED CONTENT

In addition to hiding content, you sometimes need to insert content into your pages via CSS. A perfect example of this is in forms. Imagine you're laying out a form and can't decide whether you want colons after the field labels. Rather than adding them to the markup directly, you could simply generate them in with CSS.

```
label::after {
  content: ":";
}
```

That way you can easily remove the colons later if you decide you don't like them. NPR uses generated content in a pretty ingenious way on its site: The generated content allows data tables to be linearized on small screens.[39] NPR does this through a clever combination of data attributes and generated content.

In the HTML, NPR adds a `data-title` attribute to each table cell. The contents of this attribute match the column header for that cell. Here's a sample row:

---

38 http://perma.cc/2877-49JK

39 http://perma.cc/5LWG-8KKT

```
<tr>
  <td data-title="Category">Total (16 years and
      over)</td>
  <td data-title="January">6.6</td>
  <td data-title="February">6.7</td>
  <td data-title="March">6.7</td>
</tr>
```

On the CSS end, inside a media query, NPR converts all table cells, rows, and so on, to display: block so they stack on top of one another. Then it hides the contents of the thead and uses generated content to insert the column headers before the contents of each cell.

```
@media screen and (max-width: 480px) {
  table, tbody {
    display: block;
    width: 100%;
  }
  thead {
    display: none;
  }
  tr, th, td {
    display: block;
    padding: 0;
    text-align: left;
    white-space: normal;
  }
  th[data-title]::before,
  td[data-title]::before {
    content: attr(data-title) ":\00A0";
    font-weight: bold;
  }
}
```

That last rule set is where the magic happens: The value of the data-title attribute is inserted into the cell, followed by a colon and a space (\00A0 is hexadecimal for a space).

Now you might be wondering why, after all I did to badmouth `display: none`, NPR is using it for hiding the `thead`. They are rendering the `thead` inaccessible on purpose, because generated content is exposed to assistive technology. If the `thead` was also available, the column header contents could be read out multiple times.

Why would generated content be read by assistive technology? It's coming from CSS, which means it's *presentational*, right? Yes, that's absolutely true, and I'm right there with you. It used to be that generated content was not exposed to assistive technology, but sadly, as with `visibility: hidden` and `display: none`, designers didn't understand that generated content was intended to be for presentational content only—they started using it for important page content too. To avoid causing issues for people who depend on assistive technologies, browsers began exposing generated content as though it was real content in the page. It's still not selectable with a mouse or keyboard, though.

CONSIDER THE EXPERIENCE WITH ALTERNATE MEDIA AND INPUTS

The Web is unlike any other medium we've encountered thus far. It isn't print, television, radio, a video game, a kiosk, or an application, but it functions as a hybrid of all these things and more. Realizing this, the W3C added the ability to target styles to a specific medium. I took advantage of that capability earlier in an `@media` block, but you're probably more familiar with using media declarations with linked or embedded style sheets (using the `media` attribute).

The W3C maintains the list of approved media types but is open to adding to it as technology evolves. Currently, the list addresses CSS's application on the computer screen, in print, on televisions, on handheld devices (which, sadly, no browser maker uses), and in assistive contexts such as screen readers, braille printers, and touch-feedback devices. Without a specific media designation, the browser assumes the screen media type.

At their most basic, media assignments use a single-media designation, but (as you saw with my silly refrigerator example) multiple media assignments can be combined using a comma (which acts as an implicit "or"). As I covered earlier, media assignments are also fault tolerant in that unknown media types are simply ignored, with the browser applying the contained rule sets only in the known media types.[40] Media assignments are incredibly powerful because they allow you to create layouts that adapt to the medium in which they are presented.

Design the Printed Page

One of the first great examples of designing an experience for a nonscreen medium came from CSS wizard Eric Meyer back in 2000. He showed us how to jettison "printer-friendly" pages and use a media-specific style sheet to provide a printer-friendly view of any web page.[41] He offered the following suggestions to make the print experience better:

```
body {
  background: white;
  color: black;
}
a:link, a:visited {
  background: white;
  color: black;
```

---

40 The CSS 2.1 spec (http://perma.cc/D2RD-6S7T) addresses this explicitly in the case of @media and @import but is oddly nonprescriptive about the same behavior applying to linked and embedded styles. Still, all modern browsers treat the HTML-based media designations the same way.

41 http://perma.cc/4ETE-RST3

```
  text-decoration: underline;
  font-weight: bold;
}
h1, h2, h3 {
  background: white;
  color: black;
  padding-bottom: 1px;
  border-bottom: 1px solid gray;
}
div.adbanner {
  display: none;
}
```

Most of these tweaks are focused around improving the readability of the document. They facilitate scanning and hide stuff that's not all that useful in print (such as that banner ad you can't click). You could also easily build on this and get rid of other stuff that wastes paper: navigation, most forms, and decorative images.

Two years later, Eric extended that concept and showed how to use advanced CSS to progressively enhance the print experience.[42] My favorite bit from that article was the way, in one sweet rule, he made links useful in print.

```
#content a:link::after,
#content a:visited::after {
  content: " (" attr(href) ") ";
}
```

That simple rule set inserts the `href` URL value (via the `attr()` function) as a parenthetical after every link, using generated content (`::after`).

Since these two articles came out, web designers have been granted a lot more control over the printed page. You can control page margins based on whether the page is left- or right-facing (`@page`). You can control how many lines of an element should remain when

---

it breaks across pages (`widows`) and how many can be left alone on the new page (`orphans`). You can even control where page breaks should occur (`page-break-before`, `page-break-after`, `page-break-inside`).

There are countless ways to embrace alternate media, such as print, and show it the same sort of care you show your screens. In most cases, your rules for alternate media won't be so many that they require their own style sheet, so it makes sense to put them in an `@media` block within your basic style sheet. That way it will be there as an enhancement for every browser, and any that don't support the particular medium will just ignore the block, as they should.

Embrace Alternative Interactions

In addition to considering alternate media, you should be considerate of alternative interaction methods. Technology continues to offer novel ways of consuming and interacting with websites. We, as an industry, are just starting to dip our toes—*er, hands*—into the world of motion-based gestural controls. We've had them in two dimensions on touchscreens for a while now, but three-dimensional motion-based controls are beginning to appear.

The first big leap in this direction was Kinect on the Xbox 360 (and later, Windows and Xbox One). The Kinect watches for body movements such as raising your hand (which gets Kinect to pay attention), pushing forward with your hand to click/tap, and grasping to drag the canvas in one direction or another.

The Kinect was a major revolution in terms of interfacing with computers, but large body gestures such as raising your hand (or a wand controller as with the Nintendo Wii and PlayStation Move) can be tiring. They're also not terribly accurate. If you thought that touchscreen accuracy was an issue, hand gestures like those for the Kinect or the LEAP Motion pose even more of a challenge.

Interactions like this—which are currently impossible to detect and accommodate—require diligence when it comes to ensuring interactive controls are actually usable. You need to determine whether your buttons and links are large enough to activate. You need to be aware of what kinds of interactive controls work well. You also need to figure out whether there is enough space between them to ensure your user's intent is accurately conveyed to the browser.

Next-generation media queries give you the ability to apply style rules to particular interaction contexts. Here's an example of when your user has accurate control over her cursor (as in the case of a stylus or mouse) or less accurate control (as in the case of a touch-screen or physical gesture):

```
@media (pointer:fine) {
  /* Smaller links and buttons are ok */
}
@media (pointer:coarse) {
  /* Larger links and buttons are probably a good
     idea */
}
```

Of course, you'll want to offer a sensible default in terms of size and spacing as a fallback for older browsers and devices that don't support this new query type.

In addition to querying pointer accuracy, you can detect whether the device is capable of hovering.

```
@media (hover:hover) {
  /* Hover-based interactions (like rich tooltips)
     are possible */
}
@media (hover:on-demand) {
  /* Hover-related interactions are potentially
     difficult, maybe do something else instead */
}
@media (hover:none) {
  /* No hover possible :-( */
}
```

In terms of real-world application, however, no one has figured out a best practice for how all this should work on devices such as Microsoft's Surface tablet, which supports keyboard, mouse, pen, and touch. Will the design change as the user switches between input modes? Should it? To that end, the spec also provides `any-pointer` and `any-hover` values to allow you to query for whether *any* supported interaction method on the device meets your requirements, but here's a word of warning from the spec:

> *Designing a page that relies on hovering or accurate pointing only, because* `any-hover` *or* `any-pointer` *indicate that an input mechanism with these capabilities is available, is likely to result in a poor experience.*[43]

In other words, use them with caution and probably only in concert with other queries.

Think Bigger

Of course, in addition to considering the level of accuracy your users have while interacting with your site, you need to consider the potentially increased distance at which they are reading your content.

When you design your sites, you'll want to ensure your line lengths stay somewhere in the 45–75 character range. You can manage that by adjusting column widths according to the font size pretty easily. Assuming you've set the `max-width` of your responsive design for the largest size you want to design for, what happens when the screen is bigger than that? You get white space on one or both sides of the design. The larger the screen, the more white space you see. This can be particularly problematic on large wall-mounted displays.

---

43 http://perma.cc/M535-D6PX

This is where the viewport width (vw) unit of measurement can be quite useful. A vw is a fraction of the overall viewport width (a.k.a. available horizontal space). Interestingly, however, you can use this unit in scenarios that have nothing to do with layout—such as font size. Check this out:

```
body {
  max-width: 64em;
}
@media (min-width: 64em) {
  body {
    font-size: 1.5625vw;
  }
}
```

Here I have set a maximum width of 64em on the body element. That makes the width of the body proportional to its font size (which is what you want). Then, within a media query that applies only above that 64em limit, I set the font size to 1.5625vw. How did I arrive at that number? Math!

*(1em / 64em) * 100*

If the font size of the body is 1em and its width is 64em, then the font size of body is roughly 1/64th the width of the element. Multiply that by 100 and you have your vw unit. Now, as if by magic, the site enlarges as the screen size gets bigger (**Figure 4.12**).

If you don't want to turn something like that on automatically, you could also toggle it on and off with JavaScript.[44] Either way you go, however, this is an excellent progressive enhancement for larger screens and televisions, which tend to be viewed from across the room rather than across a desk.

44 You can see an example of this behavior at http://perma.cc/2VYQ-RG22.

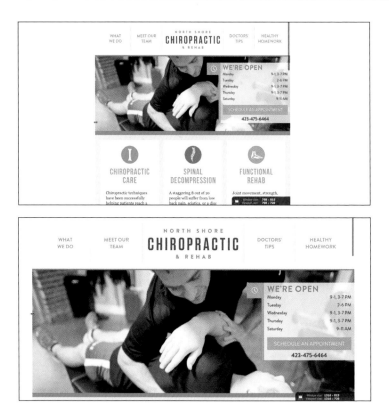

Figure 4.12 *North Shore Chiropractic (*`http://perma.cc/ARA5-JMRU`*) uses vw units to zoom its design on larger screens. On top is the narrower "wide" version below the 64em cutoff; underneath is the design zoomed in when the browser width exceeds 64em. View the video of it in action at* `http://perma.cc/MXH2-NCN9`*.*

EMBRACE DEFAULT STYLES

In his astute post "'Native experience vs. styling select boxes,'"[45] Opera's Bruce Lawson correctly identified a common tension in the web world: wanting interface controls to be consistent, while at the same time wanting them to look how we want them to look.

---

45 `http://perma.cc/YA94-D6BZ`

I've seen numerous arguments in favor of changing a browser's native rendering of interface widgets, especially when it comes to form controls. My favorites are as follows:

1. It doesn't look good to me.
2. It's not "on brand."
3. It clashes with our brand's color scheme.
4. We want the web experience to feel like a native app.
5. It doesn't behave how we think it should.

It's worth noting that browsers have done a pretty good job reducing the visual strength (and gaudiness) of their native widgets so they can blend in with a wider variety of designs. The clash mentioned in #3 happens far less often now than it did a decade ago.

Altered Aesthetics

When it comes to aesthetics (arguments #1, #2, and #3), it's true that the rendering of a native widget is not always the most appealing thing. Native widgets don't have much personality. But that's a good thing. Too much personality would lead to visual design clashes. They are intended to blend in to work with pretty much any design.

The native renderings are also familiar to your users. A `select` box on your website that looks like the one they see on Wikipedia or Zappos or their banking site will be immediately recognizable. That's reassuring. The look and feel of a `select` differs from browser to browser and from operating system to operating system, but most people use only a small number of browsers throughout the day—at work, at home, on their device. If you want to ensure the design of a form control feels "right" to them, it's probably best to go with the native rendering in the browser they're using at the time.

That OS Look and Feel

It can seem desirable to have a particular widget on the Web look and feel like a similar widget within the operating system (argument #4). That's not a rabbit hole you want to go down. Here's why:

Achieving exact design and functional parity between a native control and a web control often requires extra markup, a bunch of CSS, and a bit of JavaScript. As with the button I discussed in Chapter 3, it can be done, but it's a lot more work, and you don't get to take advantage of all the baked-in behaviors and accessibility mappings you'd get with the native widget. On top of that, the end result is considerably more fragile because it has many more dependencies.

Unlike the button example, modeling your controls after the operating system's equivalent creates additional complexity over and above simply making a custom control. Of course, you'll need to decide which operating system or systems you want to mimic. You'll need to pick the versions of each of those operating systems you plan to create renderings for as well—the design of an operating system can shift dramatically between versions, so this is important.[46] You might also need to consider whether you want to support the design variance introduced by manufacturer "skins."[47] And, on top of creating unique style rules for each of your widget themes, you'll need to write some JavaScript to determine which theme to apply. Then you'll need to maintain all this extra code over time.

Or you could use the native browser rendering, and it will just work.

---

46 The design shift from iOS 6 to iOS 7, for instance, was quite drastic. It would be jarring for a user to see an OS-esque control that looks like an older version of that OS (or, conversely, like a newer version than they are using). It's not unusual for iOS devices two generations back to be stuck with older versions of the OS because of a lack of support from Apple. And these are perfectly good devices!

47 *Skins*, if you aren't familiar with the term, are a customized look and feel put on top of something you didn't create. You could also call them themes. *Skinning* the operating system is particularly prevalent in the Android world. Sometimes manufacturers even create unique skins on a device-by-device basis.

EMBRACE THE CONTINUUM

When you focus on your content, it keeps your designs honest and supportive of their purpose. When you design in systems rather than pages, it helps you keep your eye on the big picture, ensuring consistency throughout your website. Building up your design from the small screen first will ensure your code is efficient and that your site downloads quickly. When you understand the mechanics of CSS, you can use them to ensure support for the widest number of browsers, media, and input types. When you don't get hung up on making your design look the same everywhere, you create a flexible design that can flex and adapt to the device accessing it. When you embrace the continuum, you'll find your site serving far more users while causing you far fewer headaches.

Remember, the purpose of design is to solve problems, not just to make things pretty. Beauty has its place, but a beautiful, unusable thing is not design; it's art (**Figure 4.13**).

Figure 4.13 *Jacques Carelman famous "Coffeepot for Masochists"* (http://perma.cc/8GGW-LJKH) *is a beautiful art piece but is completely impractical.*

"The Web is the most hostile software engineering environment imaginable."

—DOUGLAS CROCKFORD

CHAPTER 5:
INTERACTION IS AN ENHANCEMENT

In February 2011, shortly after Gawker Media launched a unified redesign of its various properties (Lifehacker, Gizmodo, Jezebel, etc.), users visiting those sites were greeted by a blank stare (**Figure 5.1**). Not a single one displayed any content. What happened? JavaScript happened. Or, more accurately, JavaScript *didn't* happen.[1]

In architecting its new platform, Gawker Media had embraced JavaScript as the delivery mechanism for its content. It would send a hollow HTML shell to the browser and then load the actual page content via JavaScript. The common wisdom was that this approach would make these sites appear more "app like" and "modern." But on launch day, a single error in the JavaScript code running the platform brought the system to its knees. That one solitary error caused a lengthy "site outage"—I use that term liberally because the servers were actually still working—for every Gawker property and lost the company countless page views and ad impressions.

---

1   http://perma.cc/B7KR-HWLM

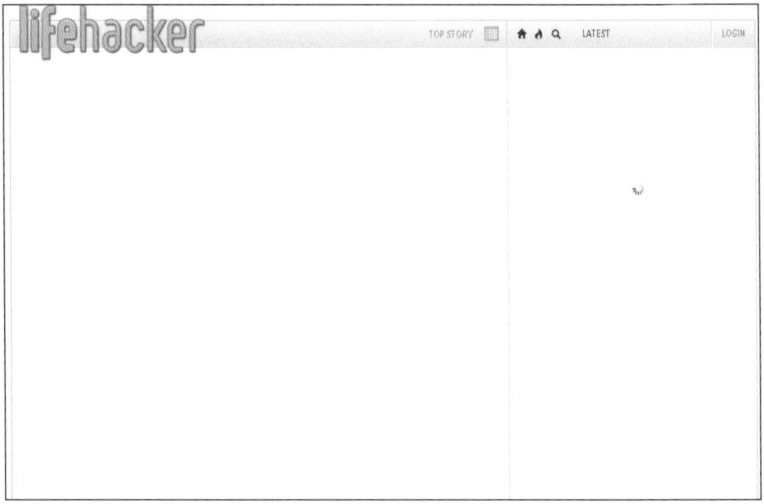

Figure 5.1 *Lifehacker during the JavaScript incident of 2011.*

It's worth noting that, in the intervening years, Gawker Media has updated its sites to deliver content in the absence of JavaScript.

■   ■   ■

Late one night in January 2014 the "parental filter" used by Sky Broadband—one of the UK's largest ISPs (Internet service providers)—began classifying code.jquery.com as a "malware and phishing" website.[2] The jQuery CDN (content delivery network) is at that URL. No big deal—jQuery is only the JavaScript library that nearly three-quarters of the world's top 10,000 websites rely on to make their web pages work.

With the domain so mischaracterized, Sky's firewall leapt into action and began "protecting" the vast majority of their customers from this "malicious" code. All of a sudden, huge swaths of the Web abruptly stopped working for every Sky Broadband customer who had not specifically opted out of this protection. Any site that

2   http://perma.cc/KRX9-V82T

relied on CDN's copy of jQuery to load content, display advertising, or enable interactions was dead in the water—through no fault
of their own.

■   ■   ■

In September 2014, Ars Technica revealed that Comcast was
injecting self-promotional advertising into websites served via
its Wi-Fi hotspots.[3] Such injections are effectively a man-in-the-
middle attack,[4] creating a situation that had the potential to break
a website. As security expert Dan Kaminsky put it this way:

> [Y]ou no longer know, as a website developer, precisely what code
> is running in browsers out there. You didn't send it, but your
> customers received it.

Comcast isn't the only organization that does this. Hotels, airports,
and other "free" Wi-Fi providers routinely inject advertising and
other code into websites that pass through their networks.

■   ■   ■

Many web designers and developers mistakenly believe that
JavaScript support is a given or that issues with JavaScript drifted
off with the decline of IE 8, but these three stories are all recent,
and none of them concerned a browser support issue. If these
stories tell you anything, it's that you need to develop the 1964
Chrysler Imperial[5] of websites—sites that soldier on even when
they are getting pummeled from all sides. After all, devices,
browsers, plugins, servers, networks, and even the routers that
ultimately deliver your sites all have a say in how (and what)
content actually gets to your users.

---

3   http://perma.cc/E53Y-LL39

4   http://perma.cc/RB97-MENZ

5   The 1964 Chrysler Imperial is a bit of a legend. It's one of the few cars that
    has actually been outright banned from "demolition derby" events because
    it's practically indestructible.

GET FAMILIAR WITH POTENTIAL ISSUES SO YOU CAN AVOID THEM

It seems that nearly every other week a new JavaScript framework comes out, touting a new approach that is going to "revolutionize" the way we build websites. Frameworks such as Angular, Ember, Knockout, and React do away with the traditional model of browsers navigating from page to page of server-generated content. Instead, these frameworks completely take over the browser and handle all the requests to the server, usually fetching bits and pieces of content a few at a time to control the whole experience end to end. No more page refreshes. No more waiting.

There's just one problem: Without JavaScript, nothing happens.

No, I'm not here to tell you that you shouldn't use JavaScript.[6] I think JavaScript is an incredibly useful tool, and I absolutely believe it can make your users' experiences better…when it's used wisely.

Understand Your Medium

In the early days of the Web, "proper" software developers shied away from JavaScript. Many viewed it as a "toy" language (and felt similarly about HTML and CSS). It wasn't as powerful as Java or Perl or C in their minds, so it wasn't really worth learning. In the intervening years, however, JavaScript has changed a lot.

Many of these developers began paying attention to JavaScript in the mid-2000s when Ajax became popular. But it wasn't until a few years later that they began bringing their talents to the Web in droves, lured by JavaScript frameworks and their promise of a more traditional development experience for the Web. This, overall, is a good thing—we need more people working on the Web to make it better. The one problem I've seen, however, is the

---

6   It would be a short chapter if I did.

fundamental disconnect traditional software developers seem to have with the way deploying code on the Web works.

In traditional software development, you have some say in the execution environment. On the Web, you don't. I'll explain. If I'm writing server-side software in Python or Rails or even PHP, one of two things is true:

- I control the server environment, including the operating system, language versions, and packages.
- I don't control the server environment, *but* I have knowledge of it and can author my program accordingly so it will execute as anticipated.

In the more traditional installed software world, you can similarly control the environment by placing certain restrictions on what operating systems your code supports and what dependencies you might have (such as available hard drive space or RAM). You provide that information up front, and your potential users can choose your software—or a competing product—based on what will work for them.

On the Web, however, all bets are off. The Web is ubiquitous. The Web is messy. And, as much as I might like to control a user's experience down to the pixel, I understand that it's never going to happen because that isn't the way the Web works. The frustration I sometimes feel with my lack of control is also incredibly liberating and pushes me to come up with more creative approaches. Unfortunately, traditional software developers who are relatively new to the Web have not come to terms with this yet. It's understandable; it took me a few years as well.

You do not control the environment executing your JavaScript code, interpreting your HTML, or applying your CSS. Your users control the device (and, thereby, its processor speed, RAM, etc.). Depending on the device, your users might choose the operating system, browser, and browser version they use. Your users can decide which add-ons they use in the browser. Your users can shrink or enlarge the fonts used to display your site. And the Internet providers sit between you and your users, dictating the network speed, regulating the latency, and ultimately controlling how (and what part of) your content makes it into their browser. All you can do is author a compelling, adaptive experience and then cross your fingers and hope for the best.

The fundamental problem with viewing JavaScript as a given—which these frameworks do—is that it creates the illusion of control. It's easy to rationalize this perspective when you have access to the latest and greatest hardware and a speedy and stable connection to the Internet. If you never look outside of the bubble of our industry, you might think every one of your users is so well-equipped. Sure, if you are building an internal web app, you might be able to dictate the OS/browser combination for all your users and lock down their machines to prevent them from modifying any settings, but that's not the reality on the open Web. The fact is that you can't absolutely rely on the availability of any specific technology when it comes to delivering your website to the world.

It's critical to craft your website's experiences to work in any situation by being intentional in how you use specific technologies, such as JavaScript. Take advantage of their benefits while simultaneously understanding that their availability is not guaranteed. That's progressive enhancement.

The history of the Web is littered with JavaScript disaster stories. That doesn't mean you shouldn't use JavaScript or that it's inherently bad. It simply means you need to be smart about your approach to using it. You need to build robust experiences that allow users to do what they need to do quickly and easily, even if your carefully crafted, incredibly well-designed JavaScript-driven interface can't run.

Why No JavaScript?

Often the term *progressive enhancement* is synonymous with "no JavaScript." If you've read this far, I hope you understand that this is only one small part of the puzzle. Millions of the Web's users have JavaScript. Most browsers support it, and few users ever turn it off. You can—and indeed should—use JavaScript to build amazing, engaging experiences on the Web.

If it's so ubiquitous, you may well wonder why you should worry about the "no JavaScript" scenario at all. I hope the stories I shared earlier shed some light on that, but if they weren't enough to convince you that you need a "no JavaScript" strategy, consider this: The U.K.'s GDS (Government Digital Service) ran an experiment to determine how many of its users did not receive JavaScript-based enhancements, and it discovered that number to be 1.1 percent, or 1 in every 93 users.[7, 8] For an ecommerce site like Amazon, that's 1.75 million people a month, which is a huge number.[9] But that's not the interesting bit.

First, a little about GDS's methodology. It ran the experiment on a high-traffic page that drew from a broad audience, so it was a live sample which was more representative of the true picture, meaning the numbers weren't skewed by collecting information only from a subsection of its user base. The experiment itself boiled down to three images:

- A baseline image included via an `img` element
- An `img` contained within a `noscript` element
- An image that would be loaded via JavaScript

The `noscript` element, if you are unfamiliar, is meant to encapsulate content you want displayed when JavaScript is unavailable. It provides a clean way to offer an alternative experience in "no JavaScript" scenarios. When JavaScript is available, the browser ignores the contents of the `noscript` element entirely.

7 http://perma.cc/5SBR-58CD

8 A recent Pew Research study pegged the JavaScript-deprived percentage of its survey respondents closer to 15 percent, which seems crazy. Incidentally, it also found that "the flashier tools JavaScript makes possible do not improve and may in fact degrade data quality." See http://perma.cc/W7YK-MR3K.

9 The most recent stat I've seen pegs Amazon.com at around 175 million unique monthly visitors. See http://perma.cc/ELV4-UH9Q.

With this setup in place, the expectation was that all users would get two images. Users who fell into the "no JavaScript" camp would receive images 1 and 2 (the contents of `noscript` are exposed only when JavaScript is not available or turned off). Users who could use JavaScript would get images 1 and 3.

What GDS hadn't anticipated, however, was a third group: users who got image 1 but didn't get either of the other images. In other words, they *should* have received the JavaScript enhancement (because `noscript` was not evaluated), but they didn't (because the JavaScript injection didn't happen). Perhaps most surprisingly, this was the group that accounted for the vast majority of the "no JavaScript" users—0.9 percent of the users (as compared to 0.2 percent who received image 2).

What could cause something like this to happen? Many things:

- JavaScript errors introduced by the developers
- JavaScript errors introduced by in-page third-party code (e.g., ads, sharing widgets, and the like)
- JavaScript errors introduced by user-controlled browser add-ons
- JavaScript being blocked by a browser add-on
- JavaScript being blocked by a firewall or ISP (or modified, as in the earlier Comcast example)
- A missing or incomplete JavaScript program because of network connectivity issues (the "train goes into a tunnel" scenario)
- Delayed JavaScript download because of slow network download speed
- A missing or incomplete JavaScript program because of a CDN outage
- Not enough RAM to load and execute the JavaScript[10] (**Figure 5.2**)

---

10 Stuart Langridge put together a beautiful chart of these at
    http://perma.cc/BPN4-5XRR if you'd like to decorate your workspace.

Figure 5.2 *A BlackBerry device attempting to browse to the Obama for America campaign site in 2012. It ran out of RAM trying to load 4.2MB of HTML, CSS, and JavaScript.*
http://perma.cc/K8YS-YHDV.

That's a ton of potential issues that can affect whether a user gets your JavaScript-based experience. I'm not bringing them up to scare you off using JavaScript; I just want to make sure you realize how many factors can affect whether users get it. In truth, most users *will* get your enhancements. Just don't put all your eggs in the JavaScript basket. Diversify the ways you deliver your content and experiences. It reduces risk and ensures your site will support the broadest number of users. It pays to hope for the best and plan for the worst.

DESIGN A BASELINE

When you create experiences that work without JavaScript, you ensure that even if the most catastrophic error happens, your users will still be able to complete key tasks such as registering for an account, logging in to your site, or buying a product. This is easily achievable using standard HTML markup, links to actual pages, and forms that can be submitted to a server. HTTP is your friend. It's the foundation of the Web, and you should embrace it.

As you'll recall from Chapter 3, using non-native controls to handle activities such as form submission increases the number of dependencies your site has in order to deliver the right experience. Using real links, actual buttons, and other native controls keeps the number of dependencies to an absolute minimum, ensuring your users can do what they came to your site to do.

Establishing this sort of baseline for a web project built as a "single-page app"—using a front-end MVC (Model-View-Controller) framework such as Angular, Backbone, or Ember—used to be a challenge. In fact, it was the primary driver for many JavaScript programmers to call for the death of progressive enhancement, as Ember creator Tom Dale did in 2013.[11]

> *We live in a time where you can assume JavaScript is part of the web platform. Worrying about browsers without JavaScript is like worrying about whether you're backwards compatible with HTML 3.2 or CSS2. At some point, you have to accept that some things are just part of the platform. Drawing the line at JavaScript is an arbitrary delineation that doesn't match the state of browsers in 2013.*

As JavaScript has become more firmly established as a server-side programming language too (thanks to node.js), it has become possible for developers to execute much of the code they send to the browser on the server. This technique, dubbed *isomorphic* JavaScript by Nodejitsu,[12] enables the server to respond to page requests in the traditional way, delivering the HTML, CSS, and JavaScript as it traditionally would (**Figure 5.3**). Those HTML pages contain links to other HTML pages and forms that submit back to the server. Assuming the conditions are right, that baseline experience is then overtaken by JavaScript, and the whole experience is converted into a single-page app. It's a fantastic example of progressive enhancement: a universally usable "no JavaScript" experience that gets replaced by a "single-page app" experience when it's possible to do so.

---

11 http://perma.cc/DP6Q-FAZ5

12 http://perma.cc/GHW9-SNKT

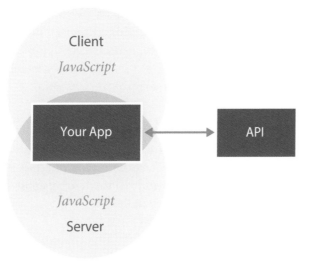

Figure 5.3 *A diagram of how isomorphic JavaScript works, adapted from a visualization created by Airbnb.*

In 2012, Twitter was one of the first big sites to move initial rendering of its single-page app to the server (although it didn't do it using server-side JavaScript). Twitter found that this move created a more stable experience for its users, and it also improved the speed of the site, reducing rendering time to one-fifth the time it took to get to the first render using the MVC framework.[13] Airbnb transitioned to an isomorphic JavaScript approach about a year later, citing page performance and SEO as major factors in their decision.[14]

In the intervening years, more sites have embraced this approach, and many of the popular MVC frameworks have followed. Even Tom Dale changed his tune and released Ember FastBoot.[15]

---

13 http://perma.cc/AE92-4UTF

14 http://perma.cc/HL7R-9ZJ5

15 http://perma.cc/27DP-NJ99

Say what you will about server-rendered apps, the performance of your server is much more predictable, and more easily upgraded, than the many, many different device configurations of your users. Server-rendering is important to ensure that users who are not on the latest-and-greatest can see your content immediately when they click a link.

I couldn't agree more. JavaScript execution in the client is never guaranteed. You should always begin with a JavaScript-less baseline, delivered by a server, and build up the experience from there. Progressive enhancement—even in the world of single-page apps and client-side MVC frameworks—just makes sense.

PROGRAM DEFENSIVELY

Unlike HTML and CSS, JavaScript isn't fault tolerant. It can't be; it's a programming language. If any part of the program isn't understood, the program can't be run. This makes authoring JavaScript a little more challenging than writing HTML and CSS. You must program defensively by acknowledging your program's dependencies and take every precaution to minimize the fallout when one of them is not available.

As JavaScript is a programming language, you can dictate which parts of your program should run in different scenarios. By using conditional logic, you can create alternate paths for the browser's JavaScript interpreter to follow. For example, you could create alternate paths based on what elements are in the page. Or you could create alternate experiences based on which language features the browser supports (or which it doesn't). You could also enhance the page in different ways based on the amount of screen real estate available to you.

Conditional logic—using `if`, `if...else`, and so on—makes this possible and is an invaluable tool for ensuring your program doesn't break. Let's look at a few examples.

Look Before You Act

You should test for the elements you need for your interface.
With the exception of `html`, `head`, and `body`, you can't assume any
element exists when your JavaScript program runs.

There are three main reasons why an element you expected to be
on the page might not actually be there.

- Your JavaScript and HTML have gotten out of sync. This could
  happen if someone updated an HTML template (e.g., moving
  an element or removing a particular `class`) without realizing
  there was JavaScript that depended on the original markup.
- Depending on when your code is being executed, the element
  may not exist yet. This can happen frequently if the element in
  question is generated by another part of your JavaScript program. This sort of issue is referred to as a *race condition* because
  two tasks are running asynchronously and you have no way of
  knowing which will finish first.
- The element might have existed on page load, but it's no longer there. This can happen if another part of the program has
  removed or otherwise manipulated the element. It can also happen if a browser add-on has manipulated the document (which
  many of them do).

Being aware of this, you can alter your JavaScript to be more flexible. Two ways of addressing these potential issues are by looking
for an element before you try to do something with it and by dele-
gating behavior rather than assigning explicit event handlers. Let's
take a look at these two approaches in more detail.

Isolate DOM Manipulation

You can elegantly avoid missing element errors by looking
for an element before you try to do something with it. Let's
say you want to look for a specific element in the DOM like
`form.registration`. You could do something like this:

```
var $reg_form = document.querySelector(
                    'form.registration' );
```

Assuming `form.registration` exists, `$reg_form` would now
be a reference to that element. But, if it doesn't, `$reg_form` would
be `null`. Knowing that, you can avoid throwing a JavaScript error
by encapsulating any code related to manipulating `$reg_form`
inside a conditional.

```
if ( $reg_form ) {
  // hooray, we can do something with it now.
}
```

The `null` value is *falsey*, meaning that in a conditional like this, it
evaluates as `false`. If `document.querySelector` successfully
collected an element, its value would be *truthy*, and the conditional
would evaluate as `true`.

Delegate Behavior

If you're looking to add a custom behavior to an interaction with
an HTML element (a.k.a. an event handler), you can use the event
model to your advantage and avoid missing element issues altogether. Let's continue looking at `form.registration` and say you
want to do something when it's submitted. You could look for the
element (as I did earlier) and then attach the event handler to that
element using `addEventListener` or `onclick`. Alternately, you
could also listen for the event further up in the DOM, such as on
the `body` element.

```
document.body.addEventListener( 'submit', function(e) {
  if ( e.target &&
      e.target.matches( 'form.registration' ) ) {
    // do something with the form submission
  }
}, false );
```

This approach is called *event delegation*, and the reason it works
is that events move up and down the DOM tree in the *event
capturing* and *event bubbling* phases, respectively (**Figure 5.4**).
So, the submit event of a form hits the `html` element (as the root
node), then the `body` element, then however many other ancestor

elements exist between the `body` and `form.registration`, and then finally the `form` itself. That's the event capturing phase. Then it does the whole thing in reverse, starting with the `form` and moving ancestor by ancestor up the DOM tree to the `html` element. That's the bubbling phase. Since the third argument in this method call is `false`, the event handler will execute only on the bubbling phase.

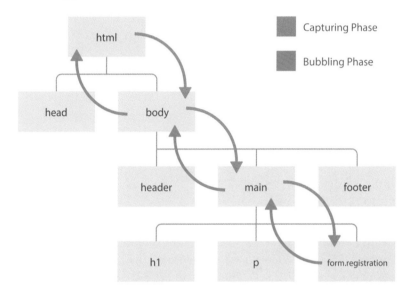

Figure 5.4 *The W3C event model indicating the capturing (orange) and bubbling (blue) phase of an event.*

The beauty of this approach is that without `form.registration` in the DOM, no errors are encountered. When it is available—even if that happens after the listener is registered—the event handler is in place to do whatever it needs to when the form is submitted. As an added bonus, if you wanted to apply the same event-handling logic to multiple elements on the page, you could do it once on a shared ancestor rather than assigning individual event handlers for each element. A great use case for this is a sortable list, where you can assign the handler on the list container (e.g., `ol.sortable`) rather than on the individual list items themselves.

The downside to this approach is that, with certain events, running an event listener at such a high level can negatively affect performance. Imagine if event-handling code had to run and the conditionals inside it had to be evaluated every time someone clicked an element on the page. Depending on the complexity, that could make the experience slow or laggy. Whenever possible, assign event delegation as close to the element you want to control as you can (as in the example of the sortable list container earlier).

Test for Feature Support

You've seen a couple of examples of where conditionals are excellent for isolating code for use with specific elements, but they're also extremely useful when it comes to using new (or new*ish*) JavaScript features. Consider this bit of JavaScript:

```
if ( 'addEventListener' in window ) {
    // we can use addEventListener
}
```

This code tests for whether the `window` object contains a member named `addEventListener`. If this sounds familiar, it's because I covered this same concept, *feature detection*, with CSS in the previous chapter (`@supports`). This form of logic is even more critical in JavaScript because, as a programming language, JavaScript is not fault tolerant. Feature detection is necessary for creating robust programs in JavaScript.

The `addEventListener` method is the modern standard for attaching event handlers. Back during the height of the browser wars, however—before `addEventListener` was standardized—Microsoft developed a competing method called `attachEvent` that did largely the same thing. Until the release of IE 9 in 2011, `addEventListener` was completely unavailable in their browser. To enable the same interactions in IE versions prior to that and in every other browser, developers were forced to support both methods. So, instead of the example shown earlier, you'd see something like this:

```
if ( 'addEventListener' in window ) {
  // code using addEventListener
} else if ( 'attachEvent' in window ) {
  // code using attachEvent
}
```

This update creates two alternate paths (or *forks* in the program) for the browser's JavaScript interpreter to take. The order is important because you could have a browser that supports both (e.g., IE 9–10), and you should always favor the standardized method (addEventListener) over the proprietary one (attachEvent). Thankfully, attachEvent was removed from IE in version 11, so it will soon be a thing of the past, but this is still a good example of feature detection.

It's worth noting that some features are challenging to test. Sometimes browsers offer partial support for new feature or have otherwise incomplete implementations. In these cases, browsers may lie about or somehow misrepresent their support when you only test for the existence of an object or method. For instance, currently Safari understands HTML5 form validation (i.e., it pays attention to required attributes, pattern, etc.), and it can tell you, via the JavaScript API, that a field is not valid, but it won't stop the form from being submitted.[16] Testing for support of the required attribute, for instance, doesn't give you the full picture. In cases like this, your tests need to be more robust. For example, you might need to try using the feature or setting the property and then test to see whether the outcome is what you expected. Whole JavaScript libraries have been developed to assist you with more complex feature detection. Modernizr[17] is probably the most popular and fully featured of these testing libraries.

Feature detection enables you to isolate blocks of code that have a particular feature dependency without running the risk of causing the interpreter to fail. A JavaScript error, you'll recall, was what took

---

16 http://perma.cc/8MR5-MVRF
17 http://perma.cc/BF8D-RS5S

down Gawker Media's whole network of sites. Feature detection is another way to reduce the likelihood that will happen on your site.

Make Sure Libraries Are There

One of the critical flaws of so many sites that succumbed to the Sky Broadband jQuery fiasco is that their code did not test to make sure the jQuery library had loaded before trying to run. You see this pattern a lot in jQuery plugins and example code, but this is a potential issue for any JavaScript library.

The HTML5 Boilerplate[18] uses an interesting approach to maximize the potential for properly loading jQuery.

```
<script src="http://ajax.googleapis.com/ajax/libs/
➥ jquery/1/jquery.min.js"></script>
<script>window.jQuery || document.write('<script
➥ src="js/vendor/jquery-1.min.js"><\/script>')</
➥ script>
```

The first `script` element attempts to download jQuery from Google's CDN. The second `script` element contains JavaScript to test whether the `jQuery` object is available. If it isn't (which means the CDN version of jQuery didn't load), the JavaScript writes in a third `script` element pointing to a copy that exists locally on the server. The reasoning behind this approach is that when many sites use this pattern, there's a good chance your users already have a version of jQuery from the Google CDN in their cache. That means it won't need to be downloaded again (leading to faster page load). The CDN version will be requested if they don't have it, and if that request fails, the copy stored on the domain's server will be used. This is a really well-thought-out pattern.

That said, it's still possible that jQuery (or whatever library you use this pattern with) might not be available. Perhaps the user lost all

---

18 http://perma.cc/V53X-HXVR

network connectivity while going through a tunnel or walking out of their mobile provider's coverage zone; life happens, and you need to plan accordingly. So, before you attempt to use a library in your JavaScript, test to make sure it's there. You could, for instance, include something like this at the top of your jQuery-dependent script:

```
if ( typeof(jQuery) == 'undefined' ) {
  return;
}
```

That would cause the program to exit if jQuery isn't available. With simple tests such as this in place, you can rest assured that your users can meet the minimum dependency requirements your JavaScript program has before their absence causes a problem.

ESTABLISH MINIMUM REQUIREMENTS FOR ENHANCEMENT

The BBC uses feature detection in an interesting way. It runs tests for several features at once and uses them to infer the caliber of browser it's dealing with.

```
if ( 'querySelector' in document &&
     'localStorage' in window &&
     'addEventListener' in window ) {
  // an "HTML5" browser
}
```

This conditional checks to see whether all three tests return true before executing the program within the curly braces. If the browser passes these tests—the BBC calls that "cutting the mustard"[19]—it goes ahead and loads the JavaScript enhancements. If not, it doesn't bother.

19 http://perma.cc/JC9U-AHW5

There's a reason the BBC has chosen these three specific feature tests.

- `document.querySelector`: The code for finding elements (so you can then do something with them) takes up a sizable chunk of any JavaScript library. If a browser supports CSS-based selection, that simplifies the code needed to do it and makes it unnecessary to have as part of the library (thereby saving you in both file size and program performance).
- `window.addEventListener`: I talked about this one already. Event handling is the other major component of nearly every JavaScript library. When you no longer need to support two different event systems, your program can get even smaller.
- `window.localStorage`: This feature allows you to store content locally in the browser so you can pluck it out later. Its availability can aid in performance-tuning a site and dealing with intermittent network connectivity.

Each project is different and has different requirements. Your project may not use `localStorage`, for instance, so this bit of logic might not be appropriate for you, but the idea is a sound one. If you want to focus your efforts on enhancing the experience for folks who have the language features you want to use, test for each before you use them. Never assume that because one feature is supported, another one must be as well; there's no guarantee.

It's worth noting that you can use an approach such as this to establish a minimum level of support and then test for additional features within your JavaScript program when you want to use them. That allows you to deliver enhancements in an *à la carte* fashion—delivering only the ones that each specific user can actually use.

Finding ways to avoid introducing your own JavaScript errors is the first step toward ensuring that the awesome progressive enhancements you've created stand any chance of making it to your users.

CUT YOUR LOSSES

Some browsers, particularly older versions of IE, can be problematic when it comes to JavaScript. The event model differences are just one example of the forks you need in your code to accommodate them. Sometimes it's best to avoid delivering JavaScript to these browsers at all. Thankfully, there's an easy way to do this using another proprietary Microsoft technology: Conditional Comments.[20] Conditional Comments are exactly what you'd expect: a specifically formatted HTML comment that is interpreted by IE but is ignored by all other browsers (because it's a comment). Here's a simple example:

```
<!--[if lte IE 6]>
  Only IE 6 and earlier see this text.
<![endif]-->
```

This appears as merely a comment to any non-IE browser because it starts with `<!--`. IE, however, evaluates the conditional before deciding what to do with the contents (in this case, delivering them to IE 6 and older). Conditional Comments work in IE 9 and earlier; Microsoft stopped supporting them in IE 10.

But wait, I was talking about *hiding* content from older versions of IE, not showing it to them. Interestingly, you can do that too. The code is just slightly more complex.

```
<!--[if gte IE 8]><!-->
  IE 8+ and all non-IE browsers see this text.
<!--<![endif]-->
```

To break this down for you, a comment is started by the `<!--`. If the browser supports Conditional Comments, the condition is evaluated. If it evaluates as true, the contents are revealed. For browsers that don't support Conditional Comments, the contents need to be revealed too, so the opening bit of the Conditional

Comment needs to be closed with `-->`. Sadly, browsers that support Conditional Comments will display the `-->` as text, but putting `<!` first hides it (as a comment). Next up is the content that will be exposed in IE 8+ and all other browsers. Finally, the last line closes the Conditional Comment, hiding its nonstandard syntax from other browsers by putting it in a comment using `<!--`. *Phew!*

Taken all together, you can use this setup to avoid delivering JavaScript to older/problematic versions of IE altogether:

```
<!--[if gte IE 9]><!-->
  <script src="enhancements.js"></script>
<!--<![endif]-->
```

With this code in place, your JavaScript would be delivered to IE 9–11, Microsoft Edge, and every other browser. IE 8 and older would get the "no JavaScript" experience. Since you intentionally designed an experience for that scenario—*you did, right?*—your users can still do what they need to do. As an added bonus, you're spared the headache of trying to debug your JavaScript in those browsers. It's yet another perfect example of supporting as many users as you can while optimizing the experience for folks with more capable browsers.

BUILD WHAT YOU NEED

As I mentioned in Chapter 3, AlzForum uses a tabbed interface, but the baseline markup is not the markup required for a tabbed interface. The baseline markup is simply a container that is classified as a *tabbed interface*. The JavaScript program it uses[21] looks for any elements classified in such a way and then builds a tabbed interface dynamically, based on their contents.

---

21 http://perma.cc/E58X-R522

By reading in the contents and parsing the document outline, the script generates the following:

- A container for the tabs
- As many tabs as are necessary
- As many content panels as are necessary

It assigns the appropriate `role` values to make the interface appear as a tabbed interface to assistive technology: `tablist`, `tab`, and `tabpanel`, respectively.

The program uses another set of ARIA attributes to establish relationships between the related elements. First, it adds `aria-controls` to the tab. The `aria-controls` attribute indicates that the tab *controls* the element referenced in the value of the attribute. In this case, the attribute's value is set to reference the `id` the program generated onto the corresponding content panel. Second, it adds an `aria-describedby` attribute that operates just like `aria-controls` but indicates that the tab is described by the contents within the referenced content panel.

To make the connection in the other direction, each content panel is given an `aria-labelledby` attribute with a value pointing to the `id` generated onto the corresponding tab. As you'd expect, `aria-labelledby` is used to indicate the element that labels the current element.

Here's a simplified version of the script-generated markup so you can see the relationships:

```
<ol role="tablist">
  <li role="tab" id="tab-0"
      aria-controls="tabpanel-0"
      aria-describedby="tabpanel-0">Target Type</li>
  <li role="tab" id="tab-1"
      aria-controls="tabpanel-1"
      aria-describedby="tabpanel-1">Therapy Type
      </li>
</ol>
<section role="tabpanel" id="tabpanel-0"
```

```
         aria-labelledby="tab-0">
  <!-- panel 1 contents -->
</section>
<section role="tabpanel" id="tabpanel-1"
         aria-labelledby="tab-1">
  <!-- panel 2 contents -->
</section>
```

Without the JavaScript necessary to make the tabbed interface behave like a tabbed interface, these ARIA roles and properties would be pointless. As with the extra markup necessary to create the interface, JavaScript is the perfect place to add these accessibility enhancements.

As I discussed in Chapter 3, whenever possible, you should look for opportunities to extract JavaScript-dependent markup from the page and generate it programmatically. It reduces page weight, reduces the possibility of confusing users by including markup they don't need, and eases maintenance because all code necessary for the component to operate is managed in one place.

DESCRIBE WHAT'S GOING ON

In addition to defining the purpose elements are serving (using `role`) and the relationships between elements (using properties such as `aria-describedby`), ARIA also gives you the ability to explain what's happening in an interface via a set of attributes referred to as ARIA *states*. When creating a JavaScript-driven widget, these three components are invaluable. They enhance the accessibility of your interfaces by mapping web-based interactions to traditional desktop software accessibility models already familiar to your users.

The tabbed interface script on AlzForum (**Figure 5.5**) uses several ARIA states to inform users of what's happening in the interface while they are interacting with it. The first of these is `aria-selected`, which indicates which tab is currently active. When the page loads and the script constructs the tabbed interface, the first tab is active, so `aria-selected` is set to "true" on that tab. The other tabs are not active, so `aria-selected` is "false" on them. Here's a simplified example of one of the tab lists:

```
<ol role="tablist">
  <li role="tab" aria-selected="true" ...>Target
    Type</li>
  <li role="tab" aria-selected="false" ...>Therapy
    Type</li>
</ol>
```

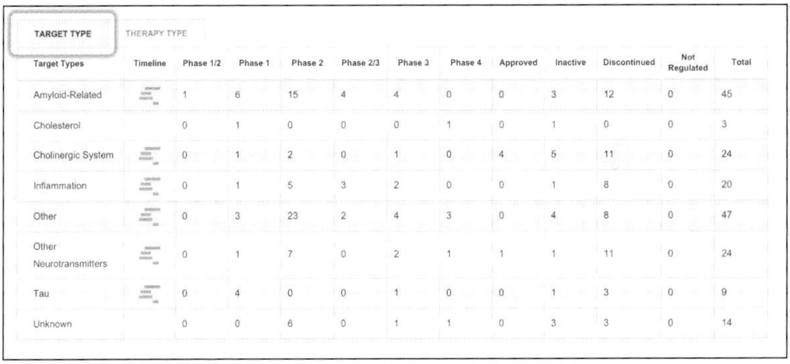

Target Types	Timeline	Phase 1/2	Phase 1	Phase 2	Phase 2/3	Phase 3	Phase 4	Approved	Inactive	Discontinued	Not Regulated	Total
Amyloid-Related		1	6	15	4	4	0	0	3	12	0	45
Cholesterol		0	1	0	0	0	1	0	1	0	0	3
Cholinergic System		0	1	2	0	1	0	4	5	11	0	24
Inflammation		0	1	5	3	2	0	0	1	8	0	20
Other		0	3	23	2	4	3	0	4	8	0	47
Other Neurotransmitters		0	1	7	0	2	1	1	1	11	0	24
Tau		0	4	0	0	1	0	0	1	3	0	9
Unknown		0	0	6	0	1	1	0	3	3	0	14

Figure 5.5 *The tabbed interface on AlzForum's site. You can see a video of ChromeVox interacting with the interface at* `http://perma.cc/89BD-TDKF`.

When a user activates the second tab in order to display its related contents, that activated tab becomes `aria-selected="true"`, and the other tab is set to `aria-selected="false"`. At the other end of the tabbed interface, a similar switch is happening but with another set of ARIA states.

When the interface initially loads and the first content panel is displayed, that panel is `aria-hidden="false"` because it's visible. All the other content panels are set to `aria-hidden="true"`. When a new tab is activated, the new panel is set to `aria-hidden="false"`, and the previously visible one is `aria-hidden="true"`.

With these roles, properties, and states in place, assistive technologies such as screen readers can identify this markup as a tabbed interface and explain the interface to the user. For instance, ChromeVox (Google's screen reader add-on for Chrome) would say the following when this markup is encountered:

Tab list with two items. Target Type tab selected, one of two.

When the user navigates to the second tab, it would read the following:

Therapy Type tab selected, two of two.

When activating the content panel, it would say the following:

Therapy Type tab panel.

From there, the user can instruct the screen reader to continue reading the contents of the content panel. It's a pretty nice experience without requiring too much of you, the programmer. The straightforward, declarative nature of ARIA is one of its greatest strengths.

WRITE CODE THAT TAKES DECLARATIVE INSTRUCTION

Declarative code, as in code you can understand by reading it, is incredibly useful from a maintenance standpoint. It can make it obvious what's happening and makes it easy for a team to collaborate.

In the AlzForum example, the developers used a `class` to indicate a tabbed interface should be created. That's declarative, but it can also create confusion, especially if there is a reason the tabbed interface should *not* be created. Thankfully, there is another option for providing declarative instruction: data attributes.

Data attributes are a completely customizable group of attributes that begin with `data-`. With that prefix, you can create whatever attribute names you want, such as `data-turnitup` or `data-bring-the-noise`. You have *carte blanche* to name them whatever makes you happy. That said, it's a good idea to use a name that's intuitive as a courtesy to your fellow developers (or you, a few weeks removed from this project). It's also considered a best practice to separate words with hyphens.

In the case of AlzForum, it might have made more sense to give the container a data attribute of `data-can-become="tabbed"` or `data-tabbed-interface`; it wouldn't even need to be given a value. The script could then look for that indicator instead of the `class`.

```
var $container = document.querySelectorAll(
                  '[data-can-become=tabbed]' );
```

There are many hugely beneficial ways to use data attributes. On Fidelity's website,[22] they use data attributes to hold the form validation error message strings. Here's a simplified excerpt from their login form:

```
<input type="password" name="PIN"
      required="required" aria-required="true"
      data-msg-required="Please enter your
      ➥password"
      data-msg-invalid="This field is not properly
      ➥formatted"
      >
```

The validation script, jQuery Validation,[23] uses two data attributes to provide feedback to users when either they forget to fill in the password (`data-msg-required`) or the value they supply isn't valid (`data-msg-invalid`). By taking this approach, the actual JavaScript program does not need to contain these messages (**Figure 5.6**), nor does it need to be updated when the wording needs to change. This loose coupling of logic and messaging leads to better maintainability.

---

22 http://perma.cc/4ZM5-PU3X

23 http://perma.cc/AK22-L4MF

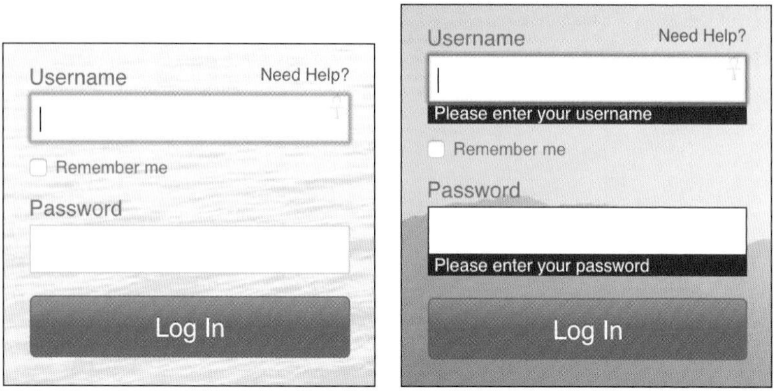

Figure 5.6 *A login form with validation error messages on Fidelity's website. View the video of it in action at* http://perma.cc/H83U-2M3Y.

Data attributes are accessible in your JavaScript via an element's `dataset` property. In the case of the Fidelity code, you could write something like this to access them:

```
var $field = document.querySelector( '[name=PIN]' ),
    required_msg = $field.dataset.msgRequired,
    invalid_msg = $field.dataset.msgInvalid;
```

Note that the data attributes are automatically coerced into "camel case"—where letters immediately following a hyphen are capitalized and the hyphens are removed—as properties of the `dataset`.

One final note on data attributes: since these are declarative instructions that are generally scoped to one use case, it's a good idea to prefix every data attribute related to that use case identically. So if you have a bunch of data attributes related to a tabbed interface, make your attributes start with `data-tab-interface-`, `data-tabs-`, or similar. This will reduce the possibility of name collisions with other scripts.

You can see this form of "namespacing" in use on the container for another tabbed interface on AlzForum's Mutations database page.[24]

---

24 http://perma.cc/M762-62DF

```
<div class="tabbed-interface"
     data-tab-section="[data-zoom-frame]"
     data-tab-header=".pane-subtitle"
     data-tab-hide-headers="false"
     data-tab-carousel
     >
  <!-- contents to be converted -->
</div>
```

These various data attributes all provide additional instruction to the tabbed interface program to configure the final output.

When used well, declarative data attributes can make the progressive enhancement of your pages even easier by reducing the initial development and ongoing maintenance overhead of your programs. Data attributes make it easier to build more generic programs that pay attention to declarative configuration instructions, and they also help you reduce the overall volume of JavaScript code required to bring your interface dreams into reality.

ADAPT THE INTERFACE

If you happened to load the tabbed interface example from AlzForum on a small screen, you might have noticed that the experience isn't terribly awesome (**Figure 5.7**). The table-based content in the content panels gets linearized for a more mobile-friendly layout (using a `max-width` media query and some clever generated content), but the tabs remain and continue to allow the user to toggle between the two different content panels. This experience could certainly be improved.

TARGET TYPE
THERAPY TYPE

Target Types: Amyloid-Related
Timeline: View Timeline
Phase 1/2: 1
Phase 1: 6
Phase 2: 15
Phase 2/3: 4
Phase 3: 4
Phase 4: 0
Approved: 0
Inactive: 3
Discontinued: 12
Not Regulated: 0
Total: 45

Target Types: Cholesterol
Timeline:
Phase 1/2: 0
Phase 1: 1
Phase 2: 0
Phase 2/3: 0

Figure 5.7 *The AlzForum tabbed interface doesn't work as well on a narrow screen.*

One way to improve the experience might be to simply allow it to remain linearized on smaller screens. To do that, the script could be updated to check the available screen width when the page is rendering (and again on window resize, just in case). If the browser width is above a certain threshold, the tabbed interface could be generated. If not, the content could be left alone or the tabbed interface could be reverted to the linearized version of the content.

This allows you to provide three experiences of the interface:

- Headings with tables for "no JavaScript" scenarios without media query support
- Headings with linearized tables for "no JavaScript" scenarios with media query support and a narrow screen width
- A tabbed interface for users who get the JavaScript enhancement and are on a wide-enough screen

But where do you set the threshold? You could set it based on some arbitrary number, but there are instances when the screen width may be "big enough" to handle a tabbed interface but it isn't big enough to allow all the tabs to sit nicely side by side. Then you have two choices.

- Keep the tabs on one line and make users scroll to see additional ones that don't fit.
- Stack the tabs.

As **Figure 5.8** demonstrates, neither results in a particularly good experience for your users. The Canon example[25] shows how stacked tabs can run the risk of not looking like navigation tools. Give Central's horizontally scrolling tabs[26] have the potential to cut off content, rendering it less useful.

The horizontal scrolling tabs could also end up *scroll jacking* the page. Scroll jacking is when something other than the expected scroll behavior happens when you are scrolling a page. In the case of some scrolling tab implementations, when your mouse cursor ends up over one while scrolling, the vertical scroll stops, and the tabs begin scrolling horizontally.

So, if neither of those two options works well, what's left? Not setting a fixed threshold.

Instead of checking an arbitrarily predefined threshold against the browser width, why not test the width required for the tabs themselves? It's inconsequential to generate a dummy tab list and inject an invisible version of it into the page for a fraction of a second to determine its display width. Then you can compare that value against the available screen real estate and determine whether to load the tabbed interface. As an added bonus, this approach will let each tabbed interface self-determine whether it should be created, providing users with the most appropriate experience given the amount of screen real estate.

Figure 5.8 *Above: Three columns of stacked tabs on Canon's page about the EOS D6 camera. Left: Horizontally scrolling tabs on Give Central.*

Consider Alternatives

So, on the narrow screen, this approach gives AlzForum's users a linearized view of the content. That's a fantastic baseline, but tabs are an excellent enhancement for reducing the cognitive load heaped on users by incredibly long pages. Is there a way to enhance the experience for the narrow screen too? Sure there is.

Accordion interfaces (like the one in **Figure 5.9**) act similarly to tabbed interfaces—they hide content until it is requested by the user. An accordion might make a good alternative to a tabbed interface when there isn't enough room to fit the tabs horizontally across the screen. A few small tweaks to the JavaScript program could make that happen quite easily.

Figure 5.9 *An accordion interface on* NewYorkCares.org.

Taking it a step further, you may recall that the `details` and `summary` elements create a native accordion in browsers that support them.[27] You could test for that option and convert the linear markup into a series of `details` elements if the browser supports it in order to reduce the number of JavaScript events running on the page.

As I've said many times before, experience isn't one monolithic thing. You can use JavaScript to progressively enhance your websites, build incredibly nimble and flexible interfaces, and provide the most appropriate experiences for your users, tailored to their needs and capabilities.

APPLY NO STYLES BEFORE THEIR TIME

When you are creating JavaScript-driven interfaces like those I've been discussing, it's tempting to style the markup to look like the interface from the get-go. That's a mistake. Continuing with the tabbed interface example, imagine coming to a page and seeing something that looks like a tabbed interface but doesn't actually work like one. That would be frustrating, right? For this reason, you should find some mechanism for indicating that the coast is clear and it's safe to apply your widget-related styles. Perhaps you can have JavaScript add a `class` or data attribute somewhere further up the DOM tree and use that as a switch to apply the styles. Though not specifically widget-related, this is precisely what Adobe Typekit[28] does.

Plant a Flag

Typekit is a service that enables you to embed any of a number of high-quality fonts on your website. The code it gives you to embed the fonts is a small JavaScript that verifies your domain's right to include the typefaces you're requesting (for licensing purposes).

27 http://perma.cc/3GZB-ZBNZ
28 http://perma.cc/C9GK-R3QF

If your site is allowed to use the fonts, the JavaScript injects a `link` element that points to a CSS file with `@font-face` blocks for each typeface. When the JavaScript program has run its course, it adds a `class` of `wf-active` to the `html` element.[29] This `class` acts as a flag to indicate that fonts are loaded and everything is OK.[30]

This approach allows you to specify alternate fallback fonts if something goes wrong.

```
.module-title {
  /* default styles */
}
.wf-active .module-title {
  /* Adobe Typekit enhanced styles */
}
```

You may be wondering why you'd want to do something like that when CSS provides for font stacks[31] that automatically support fallback options. In many cases, you won't need to do this, but sometimes the font you are loading has different characteristics or weights than the "web-safe" fallback options defined in your font stack. In cases like that, you may want your baseline type to be sized differently or have different `letter-spacing` or `line-height` settings. You can't fine-tune fonts in the same way with only a font stack.

Capitalize on ARIA

When you are dealing with an interface that maps well to a dynamic ARIA construct (e.g., tabbed interfaces, tree lists, accordions), you

---

29 Typekit's JavaScript actually adds numerous `class` names during its life cycle: `wf-loading` while it gets started, `wf-active` when it finished successfully, and `wf-inactive` if something goes wrong. You can read more about these classes and other "font events" at `http://perma.cc/4G59-LTWR`.

30 Typekit gets bonus points for using a unique prefix (`wf-`) to reduce potential collision with other "active" `class` names.

31 `http://perma.cc/JE4F-4S6U`

can keep things simple and use the ARIA roles and states as your selectors. AlzForum uses this approach for its tabbed interface.

```
[role=tablist] {
  /* styles for the tab container */
}
[role=tab] {
  /* styles for tabs */
}
[role=tab][aria-selected=true] {
  /* styles for the current tab */
}
[role=tabpanel] {
  /* styles for the current content panel */
}
[role=tabpanel][aria-hidden=true] {
  /* styles for the other content panels */
}
```

This approach is an alternative to using a `class` or data attribute as a trigger for your styles, but it operates in much the same way if you are adding these roles and states dynamically (like you should be).

ENHANCE ON DEMAND

Just as you should be selective about when you apply certain styles, you can be selective about when you load content and assets that are "nice to have." I first mentioned this concept, called *lazy loading*, in Chapter 2 in my discussion of thumbnail images on newspaper sites. The idea behind lazy loading is that only the core content is loaded by default as part of the baseline experience. Once that baseline is in place, additional text content, images, or even CSS and JavaScript can be loaded as needed. Sometimes that need is user-driven; other times it's programmatic.

The *Boston Globe* website, for instance, uses lazy loading to inject large content drawers for each of its main navigation items (**Figure 5.10**). These drawers highlight numerous stories, some of which include thumbnail images. This content is useful but not necessary for every user who comes to the site. In fact, these drawers are really useful only if a user can hover over the navigation menu. For these reasons, the markup for these drawers is lazy loaded once the page is finished loading and only if the screen is larger than 788px and the browser supports hover events.

Figure 5.10 *The Boston Globe uses lazy loading to inject promotional content drawers into the page. They are revealed when hovering the main navigation items.*

This approach often gets used for other common types of supplemental content, such as related items and reviews in ecommerce or comments on a blog. That said, the benefits of lazy loading are not limited to content. Web design consultancy The Filament Group wrote a lengthy post about how it uses lazy loading to improve page-load performance.[32] The approach inserts critical CSS and JavaScript into the page within `style` and `script` elements, respectively. It uses two JavaScript functions, `loadCSS` and `loadJS`, to asynchronously load the remaining CSS required to render the page and any additional JavaScript enhancements. Their approach

---

32 http://perma.cc/S94L-7B28

also places a link to the full CSS file within a `noscript` element in order to deliver CSS in a "no JavaScript" scenario. Of course, as you learned from the GDS experiment, `noscript` content is not always available when JavaScript fails.

AlzForum also uses lazy loading in a few places on its site. One particularly interesting implementation is on the home page,[33] where it lazy loads comment preview tooltips for its news teasers (**Figure 5.11**). Each comment link includes a reference to the URL for the tooltip markup in a `data` attribute.

```
<a href="node/459071/#comments"
   data-tooltip="/api/brf_comments/
   ➡ hover_comments?id=459071">2 comments</a>
```

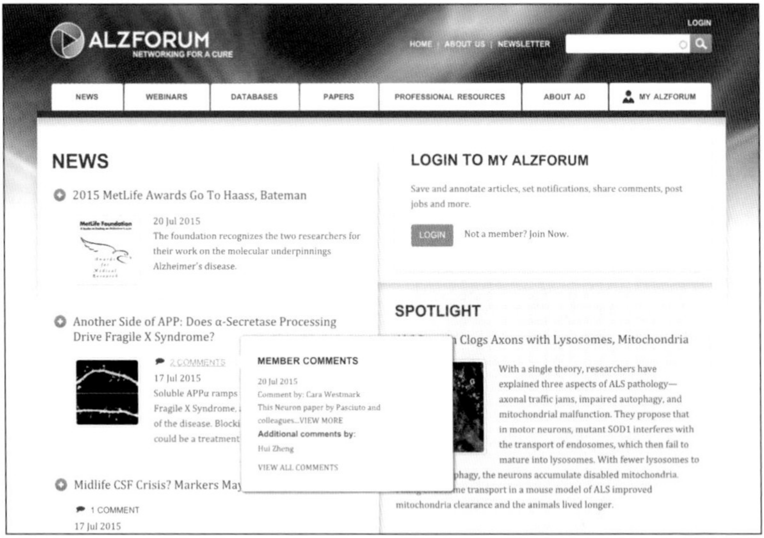

Figure 5.11 *Comment teasers on the AlzForum home page are lazy loaded in a single request.*

With that declarative markup in place, it would have been easy to write some JavaScript to load the tooltip content when a user

33 http://perma.cc/V56C-AXCB

hovers the link. To improve the site's performance, AlzForum might even have considered looking for all the elements with `data-tooltip` attributes, looping through the list, and loading the associated tooltip content in anticipation of a user wanting it. But AlzForum went even a step beyond that and wrote code that collects the data tooltip URLs and then combines them into a single request. The API responding to the request can look for multiple `id` values and return the markup for all the tooltips. The JavaScript then splits up the returned markup and assigns each tooltip to its respective link. This approach is incredibly efficient—a single request has far less overhead than the eight to ten that would be required if they were gathered individually.

Lazy loading embodies the spirit of progressive enhancement. It allows you to identify optional content and code, loading it only when it makes sense to do so. It's also an approach that drastically improves your users' experiences by enabling your website to be rendered faster. In Chapter 6, you'll explore another lazy loading technique in even greater depth.

LOOK BEYOND THE MOUSE

When it comes to interaction, we tend to be very mouse-focused. We design small buttons and links, closely grouped together. We listen for "click" events predominantly. And we often ignore the ways that nonmousing or multimodal users interact with our pages. Progressive enhancement asks us to look for every opportunity to enhance a user's experience, which means embracing more than just the mouse.

Empower the Keyboard

With the pervasiveness of the mouse and an increased reliance on touchscreens, it's easy to forget about the humble keyboard, but that would be a critical mistake. The keyboard is an incredibly useful tool and is the standard interface for vision-impaired users and power users alike. When it comes to the keyboard, we've learned a great deal in the last few years. First, we realized that access keys were a good idea in theory but not so great in practice.[34] Second, we realized that overzealous application of the `tabindex` attribute could get your users jumping (and not in a good way).[35] But the most important thing we've discovered is that we can use JavaScript to "juggle" `tabindex` values in order to streamline a user's path through a complex widget such as a tabbed interface or an accordion.

So, what exactly is `tabindex` juggling? Well, sometime in 2005 (it's hard to pin down the exact origin), we discovered that assigning `tabindex="-1"` to an element would remove that element from the default tab order of the document.[36] Interestingly, despite being taken out of the document's tab order, the element remained focusable via JavaScript (using `element.focus()`). This opened up a lot of possibilities for controlling a user's experience.

Let's walk through a scenario, revisiting the tabbed interface from AlzForum.

1. A user arrives at the tabbed interface and presses the Tab key on the keyboard, bringing focus to the first tab (which is associated with the visible content panel).
2. Pressing the Tab key again moves focus out of the tabbed interface and to the next piece of focusable content (e.g., a link, form field, or any element with a `tabindex` of 0 or higher).
3. Holding Shift while hitting the Tab key returns the user to the tab list and restores focus to the currently active tab.
4. Using the arrow keys, the user can move forward and backward through the tabs in the tab list.
5. Hitting the Enter key at any point while navigating through the tab list brings focus to the content panel associated with the currently focused tab.

---

34 http://perma.cc/HV72-F6P7

35 http://perma.cc/RK86-9AQP

36 This was especially interesting because, according to the W3C spec, `tabindex` should accept values only between 0 and 32767. Yeah, you read that right: 32767.

This is all made possible with `tabindex` juggling. Here's how this interaction becomes possible:

1. By assigning a `tabindex` of -1 to every tab and tab panel, you remove them from the default tab order of the page.
2. Going back and reassigning a value of 0 to the currently active tab restores it to its default position in the tab order.
3. Using JavaScript, you can dynamically adjust the `tabindex` value of each tab as a user moves left or right and up or down on the keyboard. You do this by changing the destination tab to a `tabindex` of 0 and giving the previously selected one a `tabindex` of -1.
4. The content panels always have a `tabindex` of -1, which means a user can focus them only via an interaction that involves JavaScript (which sits by listening for the Enter key to be pressed).

Juggling `tabindex` may sound complicated, but it's really not. In the tab-swapping scenario, it can be as simple as this:

```
old_tab.setAttribute( 'tabindex', '-1' );
new_tab.setAttribute( 'tabindex', '0' );
```

Enhance for Touch

Since the advent of the iPhone, touch has become an important interaction to consider, but touch didn't start there. We've had touchscreens since the mid-1960s. We've had them in portable devices since way back in 1984 when Casio introduced the AT–550 watch[37] and in mobile phones since IBM announced the Simon[38] in 1993. But things definitely took a massive leap forward when Apple released the iPhone in 2007.

---

37 That watch was pretty crazy. It allowed you to trigger the calculator function by tapping in the lower-left corner of the watch face. You could then draw the numbers and operands you wanted to use in your calculation: `http://perma.cc/A78S-MC25`. Could it have been the first smart watch?

38 The IBM Simon was the first combination of a cellular telephone and a touchscreen. It was also a personal digital assistant (PDA) and supported sending and receiving email.

At the time, most of us were used to designing interactions with a continuously available mouse pointer in mind. When someone browses the Web with their finger, we don't have a constant sense of where they are in the interface. We don't have the ability to sense when they are hovering over an element—events such as `mousemove`, `mouseenter`, and the like are simply irrelevant.

Thankfully, the `click` event already existed. It does a good job of unifying keyboard- and mouse-based activation of elements such as links and buttons. The Safari browser for iOS triggers `click` events as well, albeit with a 300ms delay.[39] The reason for the delay is to allow for a user to double-tap the screen to zoom.

Accompanying the release of the iPhone were a handful of touch-related events: `touchstart`, `touchend`, `touchmove`, and `touchcancel`. The `touchend` event, in particular, became a solid alternative to `click` because it avoided the 300ms delay altogether.

As per usual, we began to make assumptions based on the availability of touch. Here's an example of something I regret doing at the time:

```
if ( 'ontouchend' in window ) {
   tap_event = 'touchend';
}

/* and later on */

element.addEventListener( tap_event, myCallback,
   false );
```

Do not try this at home. This code assumes that `click` is a good baseline (which it is), but then it clobbers it as the event to look for if touch is available, assuming touch is the right event to trigger `myCallback` (my fake event-handler function). What if a user can do both?

---

39 Other touch devices do it, too. Here's a good overview and workaround: http://perma.cc/9DVB-CYRM.

You can assign both event handlers, but that's a little cumbersome.

```
element.addEventListener( 'click', myCallback,
  false );
element.addEventListener( 'touchend', myCallback,
  false );
```

Unfortunately, this code would also fire myCallback twice on a device that supports both event types—the click handler version will fire 300ms behind the touchend one. To overcome that issue, you'd need to ensure the handler is fired only once, requiring even more code (and some additional abstraction).[40]

```
// determine if touch is available
var has_touch = 'touchend' in window;

// abstract the event assignment
function assignTapHandler( the_element, callback ) {
  // track whether it's been called
  var called = false;

  // ensure the event has not been called already
  // before firing the callback
  function once() {
    if ( !called ) {
      callback.apply( this, arguments );

      // note that it's been called
      called = true;
    }
  }

  // attach the event listeners
  the_element.addEventListener( 'click', once,
    false );
```

---

40 You can see this code in action on CodePen:
    http://perma.cc/AS4P-NCAQ.

```
if ( has_touch ) {
  the_element.addEventListener( <touchend>, once,
    false );
  }
}

// finally, use the abstraction
assignTapHandler( element, myCallback );
```

Phew! That's a lot to wrap your head around for something as simple as a click or tap. What if you wanted to support pen events too? If only it could be easier….

This problem is precisely what Pointer Events[41] were developed to address. Pointer Events abstract pointer-based interactions—mouse, pen, touch, and whatever's next—to a series of generic events that fire no matter what type of interaction is happening. Once you've caught the event, you can decide what to do with it and even whether you want to do something different based on the mode of input.

```
window.addEventListener('pointerdown', detectInput,
  false);

function detectInput( event ) {
  switch( event.pointerType ) {
    case 'mouse':
      // mouse input detected
      break;
    case 'pen':
      // pen/stylus input detected
      break;
    case 'touch':
      // touch input detected
      break;
    default:
```

41 http://perma.cc/4UP8-B6AJ

```
        // pointerType could not be detected
        // or is not accounted for
    }
}
```

Pointer Events are still new but have gained significant traction. As I write this, Apple is the lone holdout. Ideally, that will have changed by the time you pick up this book.[42]

DON'T DEPEND ON THE NETWORK

More and more of your users are weaving the Web into the parts of their lives when they aren't behind a desk with a hardwired connection to the Internet. As people move around during the day, their connections bounce from cell tower to Wi-Fi hotspot to cell tower again: 4G to Wi-Fi to 3G to Edge to hotel Wi-Fi (which is absolutely in a class of its own…and not a good one). Your users move in and out of these different networks throughout the day. And, for many, at least some part of their daily travels take them into a "dead zone" where they simply can't get a signal. Clearly, you can't depend on the network to be there all the time, so how do you cope?

There are numerous options that make it possible to handle network issues elegantly, and they all require JavaScript. In fact, this is one area where JavaScript really brings a lot of value in terms of enhancing a user's experience.

Store Things on the Client

Back in the early days of the Web, the only way you could store data on a user's computer was via cookies. Cookies let you store information such as session IDs, someone's username, or even certain preferences such as the number of items to display per page, but they aren't practical for any substantial amount of content. Cookies

---

42 Can I Use would know: http://perma.cc/QQ95-6F7Y.

are limited to 4,093 bytes in total length per domain (that's for all cookies on the domain, not per cookie). They're also a bit of a performance killer because each request sent by the browser includes every cookie in use by the domain receiving the request.

We needed something better. That something better came in two forms: localStorage and sessionStorage.[43] These two technologies operate in the same way, but localStorage persists from session to session (i.e., it sticks around even when you've quit the browser application), and sessionStorage is available only for the duration of your session (i.e., while the browser is open). In both, the information you store is private to your domain, and you are limited to about 5MB of storage. I'll focus on localStorage, but you can rest assured that sessionStorage can do the same things because they are both instances of the same Storage object.

You can detect localStorage support just like any other JavaScript language feature.

```
if ( 'localStorage' in window &&
    window.localStorage !== null ) {
  // It's safe to use localStorage
}
```

You might be wondering why there are two conditions that need to be met before you proceed down the path of using localStorage. A user must give your site permission to store information on their machine. If they decline, window.localStorage will be null.

You can store data as string-based key-value pairs, like this:

```
localStorage.setItem( 'key', 'value' );
```

You are limited to storing strings of data, so you can't save DOM references. You can, however, store JavaScript objects if you coerce them to JSON strings first.

---

43 http://perma.cc/Z3LM-94PQ

```
localStorage.setItem( 'my_object',
  JSON.stringify( my_object ) );
```

Getting them back is easy too.

```
var my_value = localStorage.getItem( 'key' ),
    my_object = JSON.parse( localStorage.getItem(
                  'my_object' ) );
```

Just be aware that your data stores can be overwritten accidentally.

```
localStorage.setItem( 'key', 'value' );

// and later on or in another script
localStorage.setItem( 'key', 'another value' );
```

This isn't so much of an issue if you don't use `localStorage` for much or you are a one-person dev shop, but if you want to play well in the `localStorage` sandbox, it's a good idea to namespace your keys. I tend to prefer prepending the JavaScript object name to the key. So if I were to use `localStorage` to store a reference to the currently selected tab in a tabbed interface, I might do something like this:

```
localStorage.setItem( 'TabInterface.current',
  'tab-0' );
```

Alternatively, you could use a helper such as Squirrel.js that allows you to create an isolated data store within `localStorage` based on this idea.[44]

Client-side storage can be used for all sorts of helpful enhancements. Perhaps you'd like to store your CSS locally to improve performance and provide a better offline experience.[45] Or maybe you simply want to cache responses given by heavy Ajax calls so

---

44 http://perma.cc/MPT6-VYNT

45 http://perma.cc/W3NT-X8CA

you only need to make them once.[46] Or maybe you want to reduce your users' frustrations with forms and save the content as they enter it, just in case the browser crashes.[47]

Riffing on the form idea a bit more, you could hijack a form submission and post the form data via `XMLHttpRequest`. If the request fails (because the user is offline or you can't read the server), you could capture the form data in a JSON object, squirrel it away in `LocalStorage`, and inform the user you'll send it when the connection is back up. You could then have JavaScript poll at a certain interval to see when the connection comes back. When it does, you could submit the data and inform the user that it's been sent. Talk about enhancing the forms experience!

You could even take this approach further and make an entire web app function offline, performing data synchronizations with the server only when a connection is available. It's entirely possible. And if you don't want to write the logic yourself, there are tools such as PouchDB[48] that can rig it all up for you. With `LocalStorage`, the possibilities are endless. OK, that's not really true; they're bound by the 5MB storage limit, but I think you get my point.

Of course, `LocalStorage` is not the only option when it comes to enabling offline experiences, but it is one of the easiest ways to get started.

Taking Offline Further

If you like the ability to store structured content locally but find that `LocalStorage` is limited in terms of its power and storage space, `indexedDB`[49] might be what you are looking for. When

---

46 http://perma.cc/6E3J-6PTB

47 http://perma.cc/7AJG-GPZT

48 http://perma.cc/JQ3N-2MCN

49 http://perma.cc/KX33-Z4PD

you work with `indexedDB`, your storage limit increases tenfold to 50MB. The `indexedDB` data store is also much more advanced than the simple key-value pairings of `localStorage`; its capabilities much more closely resemble what you'd expect from a traditional database. The one trade-off for this additional power and storage space is a more complex API, but it is intuitive once you understand how all the pieces fit together.

Another option worth considering is a Service Worker.[50] A Service Worker is a script that is run by the browser in a separate thread from your website but that is registered and governed by your site. As Service Workers exist within the browser, they are granted access to features that would not make sense in a web-page context. Eventually this will include push messages, background sync, geofencing, and more, but Service Workers are a new idea and are starting with one feature: the ability to intercept and handle network requests, including managing the caching of resources for offline use. Previous to Service Workers, the only way we had to control what browsers cached was via the Application Cache, and it was complicated and fraught with issues.[51] Service Workers should make the Application Cache obsolete.

As I am writing this, Service Workers are still in their infancy, and only Chrome has a complete implementation of the draft specification. That said, Firefox is working on one, and Microsoft is showing an interest in Service Workers as well. When they do land, Service Workers will undoubtedly be an excellent tool for enhancing your users' experiences when the network is not available.

Finally, if the website you work on is more transactional than informational, all of this offline business can help you in another way as well: You can easily make your website *installable*. The W3C has

---

50 The Working Draft specification is at `http://perma.cc/4XRC-MH36`, and you can find a good introduction to them at `http://perma.cc/A6U4-2MLX`.

51 `http://perma.cc/3XAV-TZT5`

been working on the Application Manifest specification[52] to enable websites to become installable applications. The spec is still a draft as I am writing this, but we are already starting to see tools—like ManifoldJS[53]—that allow you to generate installable application wrappers for your website. These "hosted" apps already work on Android, Chrome OS, Firefox OS, iOS, and even Windows. Once installed, your website can request access to more of the operating system's core services such as the address book, calendar, and more. Talk about progressive enhancement!

WIELD YOUR POWER WISELY

Make no mistake, progressive enhancement with JavaScript requires considerably more effort than it does with CSS or HTML. The first and most critically important thing you can do is to become familiar with all the things that can potentially demolish your JavaScript-based experiences. The more familiarity you have with them, the more steps you can take to mitigate the potential damage.

Having a solid experience in the absence of JavaScript is a good starting point because it will ensure your users will always be able to do what they came to your site to do, no matter what happens. From there, authoring your JavaScript programs defensively—detecting language features and elements you want to work with—will help you avoid introducing errors when an outside influence such as a browser plugin or ad service messes with your page.

There's nothing wrong with setting a minimum threshold for browser support using feature detection; just be sure your choices aren't arbitrary and accurately reflect your goals for the project. You could even take this a step further and avoid delivering JavaScript to browsers you know are particularly old or incapable

---

52 http://perma.cc/TC6A-S2Y8
53 http://perma.cc/F2WR-H27T

of using tools such as Conditional Comments. With a JavaScript-less baseline in place, your users on unsupported browsers will still be taken care of, and you can focus on enhancing the experiences of users who have access to more modern browsers.

When you are designing JavaScript-driven widgets, don't embed the markup in the document. Instead, use `class` or data attribute triggers to inform your JavaScript program that it can convert the existing markup into a specific interactive widget and enable the necessary styles. This reduces the potential for user confusion in seeing an interface that might not behave as expected, and it also gives you more flexibility to evolve the implementation over time. Use ARIA to explain the component parts of the interface and what's happening as a user interacts with it so that your users who require the aid of assistive technology are just as well-supported as your other users. Adapt your widgets to be appropriate to the form factor, prioritizing your users' reading experience over your JavaScript cleverness.

Finally, look for ways to increase the reach of your creations by opening them up to alternative inputs such as touch, keyboards, and pens. And recognize that even the network is not a given in our increasingly mobile world. Take advantage of the tools that allow you to improve the performance of your website through clever caching and moving more of your experience offline. Your users will thank you for it.

JavaScript is an incredibly powerful tool with the astonishing potential to drastically improve or unforgivably ruin your users' experience. As Spider-Man's Uncle Ben famously said, "With great power there must also come great responsibility!" Armed with a solid understanding of how to best wield the power of JavaScript, you're sure to make smart decisions and build even more usable sites.

"The web's greatest strength, I believe, is often seen as a limitation, as a defect. It is the nature of the web to be flexible, and it should be our role as designers and developers to embrace this flexibility, and produce pages which, by being flexible, are accessible to all."

—JOHN ALLSOPP

CHAPTER 6:
CRAFTING A CONTINUUM

As you've seen over the course of the previous chapters, not only does progressive enhancement enable more users to access your website, it can also make the development process much easier on you. It all starts by shifting the way you view experience.

When you see experience as a single thing, you devote all your effort toward realizing that one single experience. With such laser-focus on that one goal, it's easy to lose sight of the fact that that one experience may not be what's best for a good number of your users. Designing a single monolithic experience is a form of arrogance.

The reality is that everyone is different and everyone has special needs—some permanent, some transitory, some contextual. Rather than striving to produce one identical, inflexible experience that serves only a subset of the incredibly vast spectrum of web-enabled devices and the users who rely on them, you should embrace the inherent adaptability of the Web and design malleable experiences that bend and flex without compromising their purpose. You can't possibly know all the places your site will go, but with a little planning, you can empower it to shine, no matter what. You can even prepare your sites for whatever devices and interaction methods the future may have in store.

MAP THE EXPERIENCE

One of the greatest challenges of progressive enhancement lies not with the coding but with the planning. It can be incredibly challenging to articulate how a single interface might adapt to a wide variety of situations. Ix Maps (Interface Experience Maps) are a great tool for helping with this.

In 2007, I was presented with a challenge while putting together a talk called Ruining the User Experience. In the talk, I discussed treating JavaScript as an enhancement and what happens when you don't.

While preparing the talk, I struggled with the best way to convey the various decision points and interface adjustments that would need to happen as a result of those decisions. With the help of my co-presenter, UX strategist Sarah B. Nelson, I decided to use a flowchart, and it worked marvelously. Not only are flowcharts simple to create, but they're also incredibly easy to understand. **Figure 6.1** is the first one I did. It was pretty rudimentary (and failed to properly capitalize the S in JavaScript), but it got the point across.

In future iterations of the talk, I expounded upon the idea of flowcharts for describing how interfaces might adapt to different circumstances and browser capabilities (**Figure 6.2**). Over the years, I found more and more ways to put these artifacts to use. And, at a certain point, the term *flowchart* didn't seem to cut it, so I began calling them *UI construction flows*[1]—which, admittedly, was a mouthful—and then finally settled on the name Interface Experience Maps or Ix Maps, with the help of a client.

---

[1]   I used the term "UI Construction Flow" in my chapter "Designing Adaptive Interfaces" in *Smashing Book 4* (http://perma.cc/68XV-HFQD).

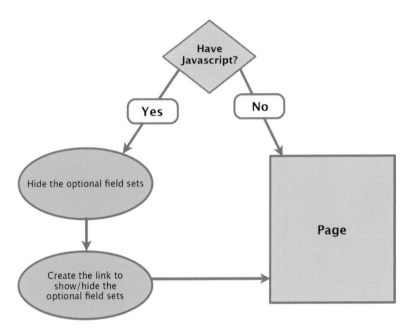

Figure 6.1 *An early flowchart used to describe progressive enhancement with JavaScript.*

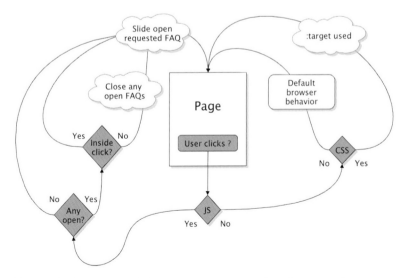

Figure 6.2 *A later pass on the flowchart, this one describing the progressive enhancement and interaction options for an FAQ.*

The Benefits of Ix Maps

An Ix Map is a pretty simple concept for anyone to grasp. This makes it a fantastic tool for enabling mixed teams—designers, developers, content folks, business strategists—to come together, brainstorm ideas, and build a strategy around progressive enhancement. Time and time again, I've seen these simple diagrams bring a diverse team together and help them quickly and easily come up with creative ways to address complex interface problems.

Ix Maps have become a useful tool to me and the teams I've worked with. They excel at articulating the different ways in which a given interface might adapt and what the end results of each adaptation might be. The clear documentation they provide is invaluable to just about everyone on the team.

- Copywriters get a clear picture of the different experience possibilities so they can craft the copy accordingly.
- Designers can see the different experience possibilities and can create wireframes and visual designs that account for each.
- Developers get a clear outline of what functionality is expected and know exactly what features and capability detection to employ in generating each experience.
- The quality assurance team has a clear picture of what they should be looking for in each component of an interface.

In short, Ix Maps ensure everyone on the team has an understanding of what's expected so they can work toward a common goal. One company I worked with found Ix Maps so useful that they created one for every pattern in their pattern library. Then they included the drawings as part of each pattern's documentation.

Because they are so basic, Ix Maps can be sketched out quickly on paper, on a whiteboard, or in software like OmniGraffle. Their simplicity also makes it quite easy to explore different ideas of how to adapt a particular interface without having to worry about throwing away an idea that doesn't pan out. It's only a few boxes and arrows…you haven't invested any time in design or production.

Example: Lazy Loading Images

In Chapter 2, I said that you must evaluate each piece of content you consider including in your website with one question: *Does this content actually add to the experience?* A relevant example I gave was thumbnail images on the *New York Times* and *Guardian* websites.

In reviewing those examples, I conceded that having thumbnail images for certain article teasers can help to draw a user's eye. This is particularly helpful on large screens where information density is high and there is a lot of competition for the user's attention (please refer to **Figure 2.4**). That said, on smaller screens, the same level of competition does not exist. Furthermore, thumbnail images can, in some cases, cause your text to wrap oddly (**Figure 2.5**). Finally, for all the benefits in terms of visual interest and gaze-attraction, these images carry some heavy baggage: They greatly increase the overall size of the page *and* each one needs to be downloaded individually.[2]

For these reasons, I would label the thumbnail images a "nice-to-have" feature, not a necessity. Let's walk through an Ix Map that illustrates the different scenarios and then discuss how it might be implemented in terms of code.

To serve the most users the most appropriate experience, you should always start with a sensible baseline. In this particular interface, the images are optional; therefore, no `img` elements should exist in the markup. As you may recall from Chapter 4, hiding images with CSS does not guarantee they won't be downloaded. You can only guarantee that the browser will not download the extra images if you don't have markup for them in the HTML.

---

2   At least until HTTP2 rolls out far and wide:
     http://perma.cc/QPA9-FWUW.

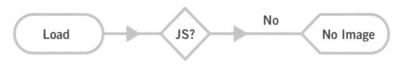

Figure 6.3 *Before JavaScript runs and in the absence of JavaScript, users will not get the thumbnail images.*

As no `img` elements will exist in the markup, you will need to dynamically inject them into the page *after* the page finishes loading. That requires JavaScript. As you'll recall from Chapter 5, JavaScript enhancements are never guaranteed, so you will need to come to terms with the fact that some users, even on a large screen, may never get your JavaScript-based enhancement. Putting these bits together in an Ix Map results in **Figure 6.3**.

With the "no JavaScript" scenario accounted for, let's go down the "with JavaScript" path. If the JavaScript enhancement can run, you want to load the images, but if you just left it at that, any small-screen browser would load the images too, which is not what you want. So, you need to insert a test before you load the images. A good rule of thumb when it comes to allowing text to wrap around an image is that the screen width should be at least twice the image width. Since your thumbnail images are likely a consistent size (or at least a consistent series of sizes), you could use twice that width as a threshold, beyond which JavaScript will lazy load the images but beneath which it doesn't. Adding this bit of logic into the Ix Map results in **Figure 6.4**.

As you can see, Ix Maps enable easy iteration. Using this document as a guide, you can begin to consider implementation details. For example, if you don't use `img`, how do you get the image in there? Nichols College, which I've mentioned a few times in this book, has an elegant solution.

```
<div class="image--lazy"
    data-image="/path/to/image.jpg"></div>
```

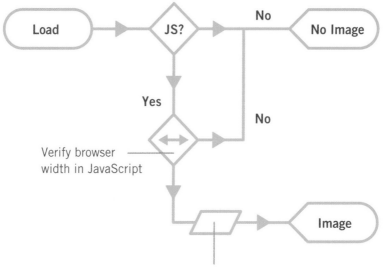

Figure 6.4 *Adding the JavaScript path to the Ix Map.*

It opted to use a non-semantic division with a data attribute to carry the image path information. This approach offers two key benefits.

- The div has no default padding or margins when rendered in a document, so it will occupy no space on the page when it has no contents.
- The data attribute makes a declarative statement about the div, indicating its purpose and offering the path that should be used to generate the image.

From a CSS standpoint, Nichols College defensively ensures the div is not displayed by default, just in case some styles from elsewhere in the style sheets might give it some display properties.

```
.image--lazy {
  display: none;
}
```

The JavaScript it uses to lazy load images is pretty straightforward. The site uses jQuery and compresses the JavaScript, but I will transcribe the meat of it to normal JavaScript with some explanatory comments so you can follow what the developers did.

```
var
// look for any lazy images
$lazy_images = document.querySelectorAll(
                '[data-image]' ),
// create a model img to clone
$img = document.createElement('img'),
// instantiate the other variables used
len, i, $container, $image, src;

// loop through each lazy image
for ( i=0, len=$lazy_images.length; i < len; i++ ) {

  // get the container
  $container = $lazy_images[i];

  // only run once per container
  if ( $container.dataset.imaged != null ) {
    continue;
  }

  // make the image and insert it
  $image = $img.cloneNode();
  $image.src = $container.dataset.image;
  $image.alt = "";
  $container.appendChild( $image );

  // mark this one as loaded
  $container.setAttribute( 'data-imaged', '' );

}
```

In Nichols College's case, rather than tying the lazy load to a particular screen width, it opted to have the JavaScript pay attention to the current CSS media query in effect. It managed this synchronization using a technique based on the work of web designer Adam Bradley.[3] Using JavaScript, the developers inject a hidden `div` into the page.

```
var $watcher = document.createElement('div');
$watcher.setAttribute( 'id', 'getActiveMQ-watcher' );
$watcher.style.display = 'none';
document.body.appendChild( $watcher );
```

In the CSS, they have a series of rules that assign a breakpoint keyword to `div#getActiveMQ-watcher` as a `font-family` value. The default is "default" (naturally). They follow this with "tiny," "small," "medium," and "full," each within its corresponding breakpoint, like this:

```
#getActiveMQ-watcher {
   font-family: "default";
}
@media only screen and (min-width:20em) {
   #getActiveMQ-watcher {
      font-family: "tiny";
   }
}
@media only screen and (min-width:28.75em) {
   #getActiveMQ-watcher {
      font-family: "small";
   }
}
/* and so on... */
```

---

3   http://perma.cc/DPW5-2CVV. Jeremy Keith did a round-up of techniques like this at https://perma.cc/MM4V-EGPR.

Using JavaScript's `getComputedStyle`, the developers then created a custom function to pluck the corresponding breakpoint keyword from the CSS and return it.

```
window.getActiveMQ = function() {
  return window.getComputedStyle( $watcher, null )
          .getPropertyValue( 'font-family' )
          .replace( /['"]/g, '' );
};
```

(That call to `replace` strips any single or double quotation marks that might be around the keyword.)

They wrap the lazy loading program you saw earlier within a conditional that uses their custom function `getActiveMQ` to test for the active media query before applying the logic. They let it run only if the breakpoint is "medium" or "full". The whole thing is then passed to another custom function called `watchResize`[4] that, as you'd expect, watches for resize events and then triggers any functions passed into it to run.

```
window.watchResize( function(){
  var active_media_query = window.getActiveMQ();
  if ( active_media_query == 'medium' ||
       active_media_query == 'full' ) {
    // their lazy loading code goes here
  }
} );
```

It's worth noting that `watchResize` also runs the passed function once when the page loads. It does this to ensure the function runs at least once in case a user never resizes the browser.

Taken together, all this JavaScript and CSS realizes the Ix Map as I've built it thus far, but Nichols takes things a step further. Since `watchResize` will run on load and whenever a user resizes the browser (an event that also occurs when she rotates her device),

---

4 http://perma.cc/WP6Y-JER9

Nichols wanted to make sure any loaded images never caused problems when a user went from a widescreen view to a narrow one. A perfect example of this use case is a 7-inch tablet—they tend to be tall and narrow in portrait orientation and short and wide in landscape. To prevent an awkward reading experience, Nichols shows the lazy loaded images only in the medium breakpoint or larger.

```
// this is their "medium" size
@media only screen and (min-width: 43.125em) {
  .image--lazy[data-imaged] {
    display: block;
  }
}
```

Updating the Ix Map for parity with Nichols College's implementation, I can simply say that the decision point based on width is actually a live test (**Figure 6.5**). It tests for enough width via JavaScript—using `watchResize` and `getActiveMQ`—and either

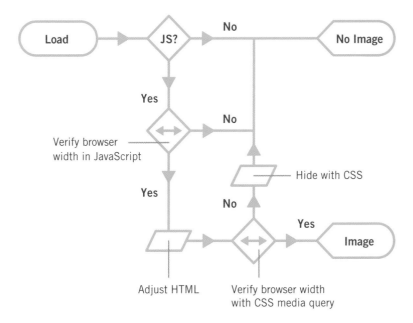

Figure 6.5 *The final Ix Map for the lazy loading image pattern.*

loads the image or doesn't. If JavaScript has loaded the image, the page then uses CSS to enforce the rule—embodied by a media query—governing whether it should be displayed. Clever stuff.[5]

Example: Tabbed Interface

We've looked at tabbed interfaces a lot and dissected them in great detail, so I won't rehash all of that. I do want to run through an Ix Map for one, however, so I can show you how this tool can be incredibly useful for iterating on an interface.

Let's say you start with the basic tabbed interface. I mentioned in Chapter 5 that you can build a tabbed interface from linear content, using the document outline as your guide. This approach is documented in the fairly simple Ix Map shown in **Figure 6.6**.

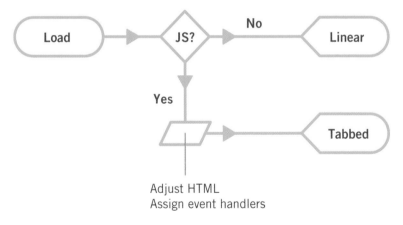

Figure 6.6 *Pass 1: If JavaScript is available, make a tabbed interface out of linear content. If not, leave it as it was.*

---

5   I have built a reduced version of this whole setup for you to dissect and explore: `http://perma.cc/F6Y3-7XKJ`.

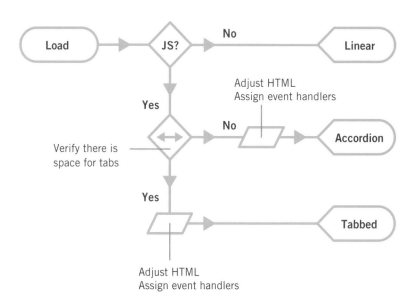

Figure 6.7 *Pass 2: Add a live width test into the mix to see whether there's enough room for the tabs and make it an accordion if the screen is too narrow.*

You may also recall that tabbed interfaces aren't necessarily the best way to interact with content on narrow screens. Maybe it makes sense to switch to an alternate interface, such as an accordion if the screen is below a specific width or if there isn't enough room for the tabs to fit horizontally. You can incorporate that option into the Ix Map and get **Figure 6.7**.

There is also a native element combination for creating an accordion: `details` and `summary`. You could avoid having to load a lot of extra JavaScript code if you allowed for that as an option in supporting browsers. Revisiting the Ix Map to include this as an alternate path would result in **Figure 6.8**.

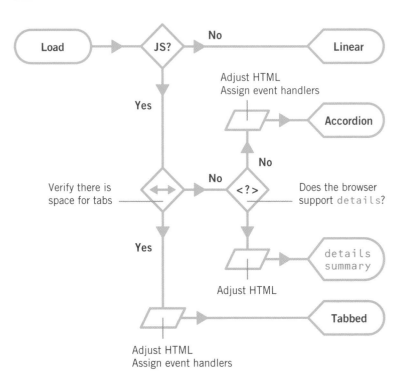

Figure 6.8 *Pass 3: Test for native details/summary support and use the native functionality if available.*

As you can see, iteration on an interface is incredibly easy with Ix Maps.

Ix Maps allow you to explore innovative ways to solve design challenges using progressive enhancement without getting bogged down in the minutia of implementation details. They are a tool any member of the project can easily understand, discuss, and contribute to. They are also a great touchstone to refer to as a project continues because they help you focus on purpose and intended outcomes. They help you visualize progressive enhancement.

LEARN FROM THE PAST, LOOK TO THE FUTURE

When discussing progressive enhancement, I've encountered a lot of designers and developers who have a hard time understanding why this philosophy's focus on supporting older browsers matters in the modern browser era. As I've mentioned at length in the previous chapters, starting with a universally accessible baseline and enhancing it based on browser and device capabilities has many benefits for the people who are coming to your site today, but it does more than that. Progressive enhancement's focus on supporting the past also ensures your customers will always be able to do what they came to your site to do, even on devices not yet imagined.

That may seem like a bold claim, but if you look at how our relationships with computers, and thereby the Web, are evolving, you'll see that looking at the past actually helps us prepare for the future.

Mobile Is the New Dial-Up

If you've been on the Web for a long time, you probably remember early dial-up modems and their sluggish 14.4Kbps, 28.8Kbps , or even 56Kbps speeds. As web designers in that era, we went to great pains to reduce the size of our web pages to deliver a speedy experience. With the shift from hard-line to mobile data connections, performance optimization has again become critical.

It seems that every day we find new and clever ways to wring a few bytes here and there from CSS, JavaScript, and images. These tactics have their roots in lessons we learned during the early days of dial-up: Keep your files light. Optimize your images. Load only what's necessary.

As dial-up access has been overtaken by broadband in our homes and offices, we've allowed our page sizes to balloon and the number of assets we request to skyrocket. We lost this knowledge until search engines started penalizing our sites for poor performance.[6] Performance matters, even if you happen to be on a high-speed mobile connection—which most of the world isn't. Progressive enhancement honors your users by prioritizing your website's core experience. Its focus on your website's true purpose will help your content reach your users wherever they are.

Small Is Big Again

When I first got online, I browsed the Web on a 640×480, 8-bit color display. It was incredibly limited. The jump to 800×600 on my next computer was huge. By the time I graduated to a 1024×768 monitor, I had no idea what to do with the space. Since that time, screens on our laps and desks have largely continued the trend of getting bigger with each successive generation. The computer I am writing this on boasts a high-definition 2880×1800, 32-bit color display, and it's not uncommon to see designers working on 42-inch screens. As technology has improved, we've been granted more real estate, so it might seem there's not much we have to learn from those small desktop screens of yore. There is.

Sales of mobile and wearable devices are quickly eclipsing those of traditional desktop and laptop computers. It turns out having a computer in your pocket is far more convenient than having to go back to your desk to look something up. Carrying around a large screen isn't terribly convenient, so the screens we have with us are smaller and more manageable. They may boast high resolutions, but they are typically packed into 6 inches or less in smartphones. Tablets get a bit bigger but not much. And wearables offer the tiniest screens of all—the Apple Watch and Pebble Time offer resolutions of 312×390 and 144×168, respectively.

---

6   http://perma.cc/R88C-ULBX

Optimizing our users' experience on a small screen—a lesson we learned in the early days of the Web—is relevant again. Your copywriting should be straightforward and to the point while still being personable and human. Your font sizes and margins need to provide a good reading experience in narrow viewports. And your imagery (if it even makes sense to include any) needs to be appropriate and focused. Progressive enhancement, with its laser-like focus on the content that matters, will help your website be successful on these tiny screens.

Text-Only Is Back in a Big Way

When I first started using a computer, few programs sported fancy graphical interfaces like we see today. The first nonconsole video game I played was no exception. Zork[7] (**Figure 6.9**) was entirely text-based. Much like the "gamemaster" role in a tabletop role-playing game like *Dungeons & Dragons* or *Vampire: The Masquerade*, the game acted as a guide for you, the adventurer. It was purely text-based, so you read about the setting you were in and typed commands like `open mailbox` or `read leaflet` to interact with the environment and play the game. When compared to the latest Xbox or PlayStation title, this kind of gameplay may seem like something that would be more interesting in a museum than on the Web. In some ways, it is. But it's also the future.

Science fiction has often been a strong predictor of our technological future. HAL 9000 from *2001: A Space Odyssey* is probably the most (in)famous example of a computer that interacts with its users largely via voice. As a concept, the "talking computer" has appeared time and time again in space-age fiction—everything from *Red Dwarf* to *Interstellar*. To function in the real world like they do on TV and in movies, computers need two capabilities: natural-language processing (to understand what we say) and speech synthesis (to communicate, aurally, back to us).

---

7   http://perma.cc/T47X-DZ6R

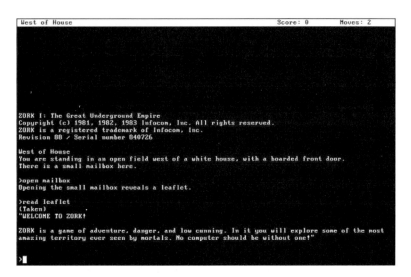

Figure 6.9 *Playing Zork, in all of its text-driven glory.*

Natural-language processing has its roots in the 1950s. In 1954, the "Georgetown experiment" demonstrated that it was possible to automatically translate a couple dozen written, romanized Russian sentences into English. In the 1960s, ELIZA began mapping text-based conversations to scripts and sometimes responded in an uncannily human manner. The 1970s saw the rise of chat bots that could engage in basic small talk, most of which were experiments attempting to pass the Turing Test[8] by convincing a human that they were also human. Around the same time, the first speech recognition prototypes were being developed.

Many of these models were limited because they were built around a series of hard-coded rules that the computers followed. In the 1980s, however, machine learning and real-time statistical analysis became possible. As hardware capabilities continued to improve and computers became more powerful, they got better at recognizing the words we were saying to them, leading to automatic transcription software like DragonDictate. Eventually, with

8 http://perma.cc/B78G-4FXK

enough processing power, they also began to assign meaning to words and could react accordingly.

Listening is great, but true communication is bidirectional. Early experiments in speech synthesis began in 1779 with Christian Kratzenstein's models of a human vocal tract capable of producing vowel sounds. Electronic experiments in the 1930s–1950s yielded some pretty unintelligible synthesized speech, but it was a start. In the 1980s, Dennis Klatt came up with an algorithm called MITalk, which was eventually implemented within the DECtalk software notably used by Stephen Hawking for a number of years. By the 1990s, reasonably intelligible text-to-speech software was being rolled out alongside most operating systems as a cornerstone component of assistive technology: the "screen reader." Notable screen readers include Apple's VoiceOver, Freedom Scientific's JAWS, GNOME's Orca, Google's ChromeVox, Microsoft's Narrator, and the NonVisual Data Access project's NVDA.

When combined, these two technologies eventually gave rise to virtual personal assistants. The most prevalent are found in popular operating systems: Siri in iOS, Google Now as part of Android, and Cortana predominantly on Windows but available on iOS and Android as well. But they aren't limited to smartphones. Amazon's Echo is a stand-alone virtual assistant that can control your lights and thermostat and order you more toilet paper. Many cars are also coming with personal assistant features. It makes sense in context: A driver's hands should be placed firmly on the wheel, and their eyes should remain on the road while driving.

Practice the Fundamentals

Over time, your users will become more accustomed to and reliant on voice-based interactions with their computers—and, thereby, the Web. Enabling them to complete critical tasks without a visual user interface will be crucial for the long-term success of your website.

So, how do you design a "headless" UI? That's easy: *You design the text.*

As I covered in Chapter 2, conversation is at the root of every interaction we have, be it with another human being, with a game, or with a website. Design every experience as a conversation you want to have with your users.

As a video game, playing Zork may seem crude and unnatural to you, but it's not. It's simply unfamiliar. Language is the root of how we, as humans, communicate, and it's likely to become a big part of how we interact with computers in the future—though via voice rather than typing. Treat that conversation as sacred and make sure that the technological decisions you make with respect to HTML, CSS, and JavaScript respect and support it. That's progressive enhancement.

BE READY FOR ANYTHING

When you use progressive enhancement to build a website, everyone reaps the rewards. Your users benefit because the products you build reach them where they are, in the most appropriate way possible. You benefit because you avoid tearing your hair out trying to give the same experience to every user who comes to your website. And your clients (or managers) benefit by reaching more users for far less money and in less time.

Embracing this web design philosophy will make you a better web designer, too. When you truly understand your medium, you can embrace its constraints and work with them rather than against them. In his piece "The Web's Grain," designer Frank Chimero nailed the beauty of progressive enhancement.

> *Most of the solidified techniques about our practice come from the natural ways of the web that have been there since the start. The answer is right there in front of us, in the website itself, and each step we take away from its intentions makes our creations weaker.*[9]

9 http://perma.cc/CV85-B43B

Progressive enhancement sees the Web as it is. It embraces the Web's solid foundation and inherent adaptability, enabling you to craft interfaces that can work for anyone, no matter what device they are on, network they connect to, or browser they use. It helps you avoid fixating on highly variable factors such as screen dimensions or specific browsers. It keeps your designs flexible enough to reach your users on the devices they actually use rather than ones you happen to be familiar with. It increases the potential reach of your site dramatically by giving everyone a good experience, even if it isn't an identical one. And it reduces your testing and browser support annoyances by selectively delivering only the code and instruction each browser can handle. Beyond all that, the progressive enhancement philosophy enables you to capitalize on the awesomeness of the Web, both today and in the future.

PROGRESSIVE ENHANCEMENT CHECKLIST

What follows is a distillation of key concepts from this book. My hope is that you will find it a useful reference in your work.

You can also download this checklist in PDF form at adaptivewebdesign.info/2nd-edition/checklist.pdf.

CONTENT

☐ Avoid Zombie Copy

People have to read what you write. Write for them like you'd talk to them. Your content should have a voice and a personality.

☐ Design Meaningful Content

Think about the content you need and what you want it to do early in the process. Content is the foundation of every experience.

☐ Craft the Conversation

Your website is a conversation with your customers. Think about the conversation you want to have with them. Evaluate each content, design, and interaction decision to ensure it supports that conversation.

☐ Plan for the Unknown

"Final content" rarely exists. Focus on content structure, and don't be afraid to temporarily borrow copy from competitors while designing your content structure and hierarchy.

☐ Write for Real People

Make sure your copy is written with your users in mind. It should be clear and take into consideration factors such as domain knowledge, level of education, and how your users speak to each other.

☐ Consider Content Beyond Copy

Carefully consider other content types such as images, video, and PDFs. Do they enhance the experience? Could the information they contain be expressed in text or in a less bandwidth-intensive way?

☐ Keep Data Entry Conversational

Pay attention to field labels, button text, and error messages and look for ways to make them more human.

☐ Don't Fill Space

Resist the urge to fill every inch with related content, teasers, and more stuff. Evaluate "extra" content to ensure it supports the conversation you're having with your users.

MARKUP

☐ Learn from the Past

Read up on the history of web design and learn from the mistakes we've made so you can avoid making similar mistakes in the future.

☐ Illuminate Your Content

Use basic HTML semantics to give greater meaning to your content.

☐ Mean What You Say

If an HTML element already exists that does what you need it to do, use it.

☐ Embrace Classification and Identification

Use `class` and `id` attributes to enhance and organize your web pages. Add microformats, microdata, and RDFa to empower your content to go beyond the browser.

☐ Make Deliberate Markup Choices

Understand the document outline, pay attention to source order, and avoid authoring unnecessary markup. Embracing these three practices will make your website more usable and accessible.

☐ Clarify Interfaces with ARIA

Use ARIA roles to inform assistive technology about the part an element is playing in your interface. But don't use an ARIA `role` when there's an HTML element that serves the same purpose.

☐ Understand Fault Tolerance

Become familiar with how to author markup-based fallbacks and use fault-tolerant patterns to deliver natively adaptive interfaces.

DESIGN

☐ Design Systems, Not Pages

Break down your interface into discrete, reusable patterns to achieve greater design consistency. Iterate on your patterns to improve adaptability, usability, and accessibility.

☐ Don't Design Yourself Into a Corner

Consider variable headline and body-copy lengths, image dimensions, and aspect ratios to create more flexible designs.

☐ Understand How CSS Works

Study up on proximity, specificity, the cascade, and parsing errors to deliver different experiences to browsers with different capabilities.

☐ Start Small and Be Responsive

Design your patterns "mobile first" following responsive web design best practices. But don't forget that older browsers don't understand media queries (and you can use that to your advantage).

☐ Focus on Standards

Pay attention to vendor-prefixed properties and use them conservatively. If you use them, track the developing standard and update your style sheets as the spec changes. Remove the vendor-prefixed versions when the standard is well-supported.

☐ Design Defensively

Provide fallbacks for new CSS properties and values. Use `@supports` to selectively deliver collections of style rules that depend on the availability of a new CSS feature.

☐ Hide Content Responsibly

Pay attention to how you hide content in your CSS and in the JavaScript libraries you use. Some methods of hiding content introduce accessibility issues.

☐ Consider the Experience with Alternate Media and Inputs

Consider how your website will render in print or on large screens. Think about how the design might need to adapt for users who don't use a mouse.

☐ Embrace Default Styles

Exercise caution when it comes to redesigning form and other native interaction controls. Redesigning native controls can require a lot of development time (and money) and may result in a less usable experience for your customers in the end.

INTERACTION

☐ Anticipate Potential Issues So You Can Avoid Them

Get to know the medium of the Web. Understand what you can control (and, more importantly, what you can't).

☐ Design a Baseline

Create an experience that works without JavaScript so your users will be able to do everything they need to do, even if something goes wrong.

☐ Program Defensively

Use feature, object, and element detection to make your code more robust and minimize potential code-induced failures.

☐ Establish Minimum Requirements for Enhancement

Consider using feature detection as a litmus test for whether you want to provide a JavaScript-enhanced experience.

☐ Cut Your Losses

Consider delivering the "no JavaScript" experience to older, less-capable browsers to reduce development time and headaches.

☐ Build What You Need

Use JavaScript to generate any markup needed for JavaScript-driven interfaces.

☐ Describe What's Going On

Use ARIA properties and states to describe complex JavaScript-driven interfaces.

☐ Write Code That Takes Declarative Instruction

Author JavaScript programs that take instruction from declarative markup to create more flexible scripts that are easier to update.

☐ Adapt the Interface

Pay attention to changes in the browser such as screen resizing, and adjust your interfaces in real time to provide the most appropriate experience.

☐ Apply No Styles Before Their Time

Have a baseline set of styles for an interface without JavaScript and then turn on the JavaScript-dependent styles when you know JavaScript is available and your widget can be used.

☐ Enhance on Demand

Look for opportunities to "lazy load" nice-to-have content (e.g., related items, comments) when users request it or only after all critical content has been downloaded.

☐ Look Beyond the Mouse

Ensure your interfaces support a variety of input methods such as touch and keyboard, or combinations of these, at the same time.

☐ Don't Depend on the Network

Look for opportunities to move critical features offline to account for network loss.

FURTHER READING

What follows is a list of some of my favorite books and articles pertaining to the various topics I discussed in this book. Some were cited, some weren't, but they are all excellent and worthy of your time should you want to delve further into any or all of these topics (which I hope you will).

Understanding the Web

"A Dao of Web Design"
by John Allsopp, *A List Apart*
http://perma.cc/J88L-BANR
See also:
http://perma.cc/ZZQ9-J7WQ
http://perma.cc/7VS4-TZRC

"Continuum"
by Jeremy Keith
http://perma.cc/U4SA-HKXY

"Information Management:
A Proposal"
by Tim Berners-Lee, CERN
http://perma.cc/EQ4P-Q325

"Web! What is it good for?"
by Jeremy Keith
http://perma.cc/YPQ4-J8CL

"The Web's Grain"
by Frank Chimero
http://perma.cc/CV85-B43B

User Experience

"Choosing Performance"
by Tim Kadlec
http://perma.cc/7RZV-DN45

Don't Make Me Think, Revisited:
A Common Sense Approach to Web
Usability, 3rd Edition
by Steve Krug (New Riders, 2014)

Mobile First
by Luke Wroblewski, A Book
Apart, 2011

Web Form Design: Filling in the Blanks
by Luke Wroblewski (Rosenfeld
Media, 2008)

Web Design Process

Designing with Web Standards,
3rd Edition
by Jeffrey Zeldman and Ethan
Marcotte (New Riders, 2009)

"Device Agnostic"
by Trent Walton
http://perma.cc/KJZ9-AFBL

Implementing Responsive Design
by Tim Kadlec (New Riders, 2012)

Responsible Responsive Design
by Scott Jehl (A Book Apart, 2014)

Responsive Design Workflow
by Stephen Hay (New Riders, 2013)

"Responsive Design is Not About
Screen Sizes Any More"
by Gorka Molero, *Speckboy*
http://perma.cc/B9MU-DFCL

Content

"Attack of the Zombie Copy"
by Erin Kissane, *A List Apart*
http://perma.cc/2RMB-FS2W

"Calling All Designers: Learn to
Write!"
by Derek Powazek, *A List Apart*
http://perma.cc/6DXB-T52G

Content Everywhere: Strategy and
Structure for Future-Ready Content
by Sara Wachter-Boettcher,
Rosenfeld Media, 2012

Content Strategy for Mobile
by Karen McGrane (A Book
Apart, 2012)

Letting Go of the Words: Writing Web
Content that Works
by Janice (Ginny) Redish (Morgan
Kaufmann, 2007)

Nicely Said: Writing for the Web with
Style and Purpose
by Nicole Fenton and Kate Kiefer Lee
(New Riders, 2014)

"Reviving Anorexic Web Writing"
by Amber Simmons, *A List Apart*
http://perma.cc/7BQQ-GKUA

Semantics and HTML

*HTML & CSS: Design and Build
Websites*
by Jon Duckett (Wiley, 2011)

HTML5 for Web Designers
by Jeremy Keith (A Book Apart, 2010)

Introducing HTML5, 2nd Edition
by Bruce Lawson and Remy Sharp
(New Riders, 2011)

"On HTML belts and ARIA braces
(The Default Implicit ARIA semantics
they didn't want you to know about)"
by Steve Faulkner, *HTML5 Doctor*
http://perma.cc/5KFU-BM23

"Notes on Using ARIA in HTML"
by Steve Faulkner, et al., W3C
http://perma.cc/M76R-VU8L

"Responsive Images 101" (Series)
by Jason Grigsby, The Cloud Four Blog
http://perma.cc/ZT6F-RZQS

"Srcset and Sizes"
by Eric Portis
http://perma.cc/G2SE-TQE4

*Web Standards Solutions: The Markup
and Style Handbook*
by Dan Cederholm (Friends of
ED, 2009)

Visual Design and CSS

"Big, Stark & Chunky"
by Joe Clark, *A List Apart*
http://perma.cc/EH8N-EC8R

*Bulletproof Web Design: Improving
flexibility and protecting against
worst-case scenarios with XHTML
and CSS, 2nd Edition*
by Dan Cederholm
(New Riders, 2007)

"CSS Design: Going to Print"
by Eric Meyer, *A List Apart*
http://perma.cc/92RE-JUTG

"The Pitfalls of UI Kits and
Pattern Libraries"
by Tyler Sticka, The Cloud Four Blog
http://perma.cc/8EHG-YQ83

Responsive Web Design, 2nd Edition
by Ethan Marcotte (A Book
Apart, 2014)

*Smashing Book 5: Real-Life Responsive
Web Design*
by Vitaly Friedman, et al., *Smashing
Magazine*, 2015

Interaction and JavaScript

"Behavioral Separation"
by Jeremy Keith, *A List Apart*
http://perma.cc/MRC5-9HZV

*DOM Scripting: Web Design with
JavaScript and the Document
Object Model*
by Jeremy Keith and Jeffrey Sambells
(Friends of ED, 2010)

"The JavaScript Framework
Bandwagonism"
by Teylor Feliz, Admixweb
http://perma.cc/HK9J-WSD3

"JavaScript Triggers"
by Peter Paul Koch, *A List Apart*
http://perma.cc/3HLG-VG75

"js;dr = JavaScript Required;
Didn't Read"
by Tantek Çelik
http://perma.cc/9BL8-J32K

"Web applications don't follow
new rules"
by Christian Heilmann
http://perma.cc/5AQY-ZXJ3

Accessibility

"The Browser Accessibility Tree"
by Steve Faulkner, The Paciello
Group Blog
http://perma.cc/7JHY-SRDE

"High Accessibility Is Effective Search
Engine Optimization"
by Andy Hagans, *A List Apart*
http://perma.cc/2ZRA-LH96

*Just Ask: Integrating Accessibility
Throughout Design*
by Shawn Lawton Henry (Lulu, 2007)

*A Web for Everyone: Designing
Accessible User Experiences*
by Sarah Horton & Whitney
Quesenbery (Rosenfeld Media, 2014)

Testing and Analytics

"Browser Testing"
by Jeremy Keith
http://perma.cc/85CN-BK2N

"Analytics confirm the need for
adaptive web design and cross-
browser compatibility"
by Jason Samuels
http://perma.cc/K75N-PFXN

"Setting a Performance Budget"
by Tim Kadlec
http://perma.cc/C78T-ECHE

INDEX